picnic hamper

Published in 2007 by Murdoch Books Pty Limited.
www.murdochbooks.com.au

Murdoch Books Australia
Pier 8/9, 23 Hickson Road
Millers Point NSW 2000
Phone: + 61 (0) 2 8220 2000
Fax: + 61 (0) 2 8220 2558

Murdoch Books UK Limited
Erico House, 6th Floor North
93–99 Upper Richmond Road
Putney, London SW15 2TG
Phone: + 44 (0) 20 8785 5995
Fax: + 44 (0) 20 8785 5985

Chief Executive: Juliet Rogers
Publishing Director: Kay Scarlett

Design Manager: Vivien Valk
Concept & Art Direction: Sarah Odgers
Design: Jacqueline Duncan
Project Manager: Rhiain Hull
Editor: Gordana Trifunovic
Photographer: Jared Fowler
Production: Monika Paratore
Stylist: Cherise Koch
Food preparation: Alan Wilson
Introduction text: Leanne Kitchen
Recipes developed by the Murdoch Books Test Kitchen

National Library of Australia Cataloguing-in-Publication Data
Picnic Hamper. Includes index.
ISBN 978 1 74045 967 9. ISBN 1 74045 967 9.
1. Picnicking 2. Cookery. I. Title. (Series: Kitchen Classics; 3). 641.578

Printed by 1010 Printing International Ltd. in 2007. PRINTED IN CHINA.

IMPORTANT: Those who might be at risk from the effects of salmonella poisoning (the elderly, pregnant women, young children and those suffering from immune deficiency diseases) should consult their doctor with any concerns about eating raw eggs.

CONVERSION GUIDE: You may find cooking times vary depending on the oven you are using. For fan-forced ovens, as a general rule, set the oven temperature to 20°C (35°F) lower than indicated in the recipe. We have used 20 ml (4 teaspoon) tablespoon measures. If you are using a 15 ml (3 teaspoon) tablespoon, for most recipes the difference will not be noticeable. However, for recipes using baking powder, gelatine, bicarbonate of soda (baking soda), small amounts of flour, add an extra teaspoon for each tablespoon specified.

picnic hamper

THE AL FRESCO RECIPES
YOU MUST HAVE

MURDOCH BOOKS

CONTENTS

AL FRESCO FEAST

Some anonymous observer once claimed that 'good friends, good food, good wine and good weather doth a good picnic make'. Whoever they were, they were bang-on the mark. A fine day that's disturbed only by soft, balmy breezes, and an open, grassy space dotted with gracious, shady trees is, where dining outdoors is concerned, about as inviting as it gets. There's something relaxing and (especially in this giddy-paced age) almost escapist about throwing down a rug, opening up a groaning picnic hamper then sprawling in the sun and casually picking through its contents. Practically everything tastes better consumed outdoors, from sausage rolls, raised pork pie and quiche to 'smarter' fare like smoked trout puffs, papaya and prawn salad and almond friands. The stereotypical picnic, which generally involves the packing up and transporting of suitably sturdy food to some location (a park, the beach or a pretty field for instance), with all the attendant gadgets and gear (such as thermoses, plastic cutlery and plates, and folding chairs), is always a treat but it doesn't have to offer the only opportunity for dining outdoors. Many occasions, from christening parties to cocktail bashes to Christmas lunches, and all the anniversaries, birthdays and no-reason-at-all revelries in between, can be celebrated al fresco.

Food that is best suited to out-of-doors consumption is that which can be easily picked up and eaten out of hand, or served without fanfare from bowls or platters. It shouldn't be tricksy, fragile or require complex presentation in order to look good — the secret of dining outdoors is in choosing dishes that can be cooked and assembled ahead of time. Whether you're a picnic traditionalist or a cook who loves to host outdoor gatherings of a casual, contemporary sort, there's everything you'll ever need in the specially chosen recipes of *Picnic Hamper*.

FINGER FOOD

SWEET AND SALTY NUTS

250 g (9 oz/1²/₃ cups) blanched almonds
250 g (9 oz/2¹/₂ cups) pecans
55 g (2 oz/¹/₄ cup) sugar
1 teaspoon ground cinnamon
pinch ground cloves
¹/₂ teaspoon curry powder
¹/₄ teaspoon ground cumin

SERVES 6–8

Preheat the oven to 180°C (350°F/Gas 4). Spread the almonds and pecans on a large baking tray and bake for 5–10 minutes, or until they are crisp and lightly coloured. Remove and allow to cool.

Combine the sugar, spices, 1 teaspoon salt and ¹/₂ teaspoon ground pepper in a small bowl and mix well.

Heat a large non-stick frying pan over medium heat and add the almonds and pecans. Sprinkle the spice mixture over the nuts and stir for 5 minutes, or until the nuts turn golden. The sugar will melt and coat the nuts. Gently shake the frying pan often to ensure even cooking. If the nuts stick together, separate them with a wooden spoon. When the nuts are cooked, remove from the heat and spread them on a lightly oiled baking tray to cool.

PREPARATION TIME: 20 MINUTES   COOKING TIME: 15 MINUTES

NOTES: If you use a small frying pan, cook the nuts in batches. Cashew nuts, macadamia nuts or peanuts can be used or, if you prefer, just one variety.

Transfer the cooled nuts to tightly sealed jars or containers. They will keep for a few weeks.

CHILLI AND LEMON OLIVES

500 g (1 lb 2 oz) cured black olives (olives with wrinkled skin)
2 teaspoons finely grated lemon zest
2 teaspoons chopped oregano
3 teaspoons dried chilli flakes
olive oil

MAKES 500 G (1 LB 2 OZ)

Combine the olives with the lemon zest, oregano and chilli flakes. Transfer to a 750 ml (26 fl oz/3-cup) sterilized jar. Pour in enough olive oil to cover the olives completely. Seal and marinate in the refrigerator for at least 2 days. Serve at room temperature.

PREPARATION TIME: 10 MINUTES +   COOKING TIME: NIL

DILL, GARLIC AND ORANGE OLIVES

500 g (1 lb 2 oz) kalamata olives
3 tablespoons roughly chopped dill
1 garlic clove, bruised
4 thin slices of orange, each cut into eighths
2 bay leaves, torn
olive oil

MAKES 500 G (1 LB 2 OZ)

Combine the olives with the dill, garlic, orange slices and bay leaves. Spoon into a 1 litre (35 fl oz/4-cup) sterilized jar. Pour in enough olive oil to cover the olives completely. Seal and marinate in the refrigerator for at least 2 days. Serve at room temperature.

PREPARATION TIME: 10 MINUTES +   COOKING TIME: NIL

Chilli and lemon olives

BABA GHANOUSH

2 large eggplants (aubergines)
3 garlic cloves, crushed
$^1/_2$ teaspoon ground cumin
80 ml (2$^1/_2$ fl oz/$^1/_3$ cup) lemon juice
2 tablespoons tahini
pinch cayenne pepper
1$^1/_2$ tablespoons olive oil
1 tablespoon chopped flat-leaf (Italian)
parsley
black olives, to garnish

MAKES 440 G (15$^1/_2$ OZ/1$^3/_4$ CUPS)

Preheat the oven to 200°C (400°F/Gas 6). Prick the eggplants several times with a fork, then cook over an open flame for about 5 minutes, or until the skin is black and blistered. Transfer to a baking tin and bake for 40–45 minutes, or until the eggplants are very soft and wrinkled. Put in a colander and leave to stand over a bowl for 30 minutes to drain off any bitter juices.

Carefully peel the skin from the eggplants and chop the flesh. Put in a food processor with the garlic, cumin, lemon juice, tahini, cayenne pepper and olive oil. Process until smooth and creamy. Season with salt and stir in the parsley. Spread in a flat bowl or on a plate and garnish with the olives. Serve with toasted crusty bread or pitta bread for dipping.

PREPARATION TIME: 20 MINUTES +   COOKING TIME: 50 MINUTES

TARAMASALATA

5 slices white bread, crusts removed
80 ml (2½ fl oz/⅓ cup) milk
100 g (3½ oz) tinned tarama (grey mullet roe)
1 egg yolk
½ small onion, grated
1 garlic clove, crushed
2 tablespoons lemon juice
80 ml (2½ fl oz/⅓ cup) olive oil
pinch ground white pepper

MAKES 375 G (13 OZ/1½ CUPS)

Soak the bread in the milk for 10 minutes. Press in a strainer to extract the excess milk, then mix in a food processor with the tarama, egg yolk, onion and garlic for 30 seconds, or until smooth. Mix in 1 tablespoon of the lemon juice.

With the motor running, slowly pour in the olive oil. The mixture should be smooth. Add the remaining lemon juice and white pepper. If the dip tastes too salty, blend in another slice of bread. Serve with crackers or pitta bread for dipping

PREPARATION TIME: 10 MINUTES +   COOKING TIME: NIL

NOTE: Grey mullet roe is traditional but smoked cod's roe also gives a lovely flavour.

TZATZIKI

2 Lebanese (short) cucumbers
400 g (14 oz) Greek-style yoghurt
4 garlic cloves, crushed
3 tablespoons finely chopped mint
1 tablespoon lemon juice
chopped mint, to garnish

MAKES 500 G (1 LB 2 OZ/2 CUPS)

Cut the cucumbers in half lengthways, scoop out the seeds with a teaspoon and discard. Leave the skin on and coarsely grate the cucumber into a small colander. Sprinkle with a little salt and leave to stand over a large bowl for 15 minutes to drain off any bitter juices.

Meanwhile, combine the yoghurt, garlic, mint and lemon juice in a bowl.

Rinse the cucumber under cold water. Taking small handfuls, squeeze out any excess moisture. Combine the cucumber with the yoghurt mixture and season to taste. Serve immediately or refrigerate until ready to serve. Garnish with mint. Serve with pitta bread for dipping, or as a sauce for seafood and meat.

PREPARATION TIME: 10 MINUTES +   COOKING TIME: NIL

Taramasalata

CRISPBREAD

250 ml (9 fl oz/1 cup) lukewarm milk
1 tablespoon dried yeast
1/4 teaspoon dried fennel seeds
250 g (9 oz) stoneground flour
200 g (7 oz) coarse rye meal

MAKES 24

Line two baking trays with baking paper. Put the milk in a bowl, add the yeast and stir until dissolved. Leave in a warm place for 10 minutes, or until bubbles appear on the surface. The mixture should be frothy and slightly increased in volume. If your yeast doesn't foam, it is dead and you will have to discard it and start again.

Mix the fennel, flour, rye meal and 1 teaspoon salt in a bowl. Make a well in the centre and add the yeast mixture. Gather together and knead on a floured surface for 5 minutes, adding a little water if necessary. Divide into four portions.

Divide each portion into six pieces and shape each into a ball. Cover and leave in a warm place for 20 minutes, or until doubled in size.

Preheat the oven to 180°C (350°F/Gas 4). Roll out each ball of dough to make a circle about 13 cm (5 inches) in diameter. Cut out the centre of each circle with a round 2 cm (3/4 inch) cutter. Discard the centre, then prick each crispbread with a fork and put on a baking tray. Bake the crispbread, in batches, for 10 minutes, or until firm and dry and slightly coloured. When completely cool, store in an airtight container.

PREPARATION TIME: 20 MINUTES +   COOKING TIME: 30 MINUTES

TWO-SEED CRACKERS

250 g (9 oz/2 cups) plain (all-purpose)
flour
1 teaspoon baking powder
2 tablespoons poppy seeds
2 tablespoons sesame seeds
60 g (2¼ oz) butter, chilled and chopped
125 ml (4 fl oz/½ cup) iced water

MAKES 30

Preheat the oven to 180°C (350°F/Gas 4). Line two baking trays with baking paper.

Sift the flour, baking powder and ½ teaspoon salt into a bowl. Stir in the seeds and some pepper. Rub the butter into the flour using your fingertips until the mixture resembles fine breadcrumbs.

Make a well in the centre and add the iced water. Mix together with a flat-bladed knife using a cutting action, adding a little extra water if necessary, until the mixture comes together in soft beads. Gather together into a rough ball. Handle the dough gently and do not knead it at any stage. Divide the dough into two portions. Put one portion between two sheets of baking paper and roll out to 2 mm (⅛ inch) thick. Cover the other portion with plastic wrap.

Using a 6 cm (2½ inch) round cutter, cut rounds from the dough. Prick all over with a fork and transfer to the trays. Repeat with the remaining dough. Pile any dough trimmings together (do not knead) and gently re-roll. Cut out more rounds. Bake for 20–25 minutes, or until golden. Allow to cool on a wire rack.

PREPARATION TIME: 20 MINUTES   COOKING TIME: 25 MINUTES

WATER CRACKERS

250 g (9 oz/2 cups) self-raising flour
50 g (1¾ oz) unsalted butter, chopped

MAKES 50

Preheat the oven to 220°C (425°F/Gas 7). Line two baking trays with baking paper. Sift the flour and ½ teaspoon salt into a bowl. Cut the butter into the flour with a knife, then rub in using your fingertips. Knead in enough water (about 185 ml/6 fl oz/¾ cup) to make a fairly stiff dough. Lightly knead the dough for a few minutes until smooth.

On a large floured board, roll the dough out until it is as thin as a wafer. Cut into rounds (you can cut a small hole in the centre of each for decoration) and bake in batches for 8–10 minutes, or until the biscuits bubble and brown. Transfer to a wire rack to cool.

PREPARATION TIME: 15 MINUTES   COOKING TIME: 20 MINUTES +

Two-seed crackers

HERB PEPPER CRISPS WITH BLUE CHEESE DIP

4 sheets lavash or other unleavened bread
90 g (3¼ oz) butter, melted
herb pepper seasoning, to sprinkle
1 tablespoon finely snipped chives

BLUE CHEESE DIP
250 g (9 oz) blue vein cheese, chopped
60 g (2¼ oz) butter, softened
1 tablespoon sweet white wine
2 teaspoons chopped mint
1 teaspoon chopped rosemary
2 teaspoons chopped oregano
90 g (3¼ oz/⅓ cup) crème fraîche or sour cream
chives, to garnish

SERVES 10

Preheat the oven to 180°C (350°F/Gas 4). Brush each sheet of lavash bread with the butter. Sprinkle with the herb pepper seasoning and chives.

Cut each lavash sheet into 20 squares. Cut each piece in half to make triangles. Place the triangles on baking trays. Bake in batches for 5 minutes, or until crisp. Remove and allow to cool. Serve with the blue cheese dip.

To make the blue cheese dip, beat the cheese and butter in a small bowl using electric beaters until smooth and creamy. Add the wine, mint, rosemary and oregano. Mix well. Fold through the crème fraîche or sour cream. Season to taste. Spoon the mixture into serving dishes to serve.

PREPARATION TIME: 30 MINUTES   COOKING TIME: 10 MINUTES

NOTES: The crisps may be stored in an airtight container for up to 2 weeks.

For a variation, combine 2 crushed garlic cloves with the melted butter before brushing over the lavash bread. Sprinkle with grated parmesan cheese and chives, cut into squares, then triangles and bake.

SUN-DRIED TOMATO PLAITS

1 sheet frozen puff pastry, thawed
1 egg, beaten
40 g (1¹/₂ oz) semi-dried (sun-blushed) tomatoes, sliced

MAKES 8

Preheat the oven to 210°C (415°F/Gas 6–7). Lightly grease a baking tray.

Lay the sheet of puff pastry on a work surface and brush lightly with the egg. Cut into 1 cm (¹/₂ inch) strips. Join three strips together at the top, by pressing. Plait them together, inserting slices of semi-dried tomato at intervals in the plait.

Place the plaits on the baking tray and bake for 10–15 minutes, or until puffed and golden. When completely cool, store in an airtight container.

PREPARATION TIME: 10 MINUTES   COOKING TIME: 15 MINUTES

SESAME SEED TWISTS

1 sheet frozen puff pastry, thawed
1 egg, beaten
1 tablespoon sesame seeds or poppy seeds

MAKES 16

Preheat the oven to 210°C (415°F/Gas 6–7). Lightly grease a baking tray.

Lay the sheet of puff pastry on a work surface and brush lightly with the egg. Sprinkle with the sesame or poppy seeds and gently press onto the pastry. Cut the pastry into 1.5 cm (⁵/₈ inch) strips. Holding both ends, twist the strip in opposite directions twice.

Place the twists on the baking tray and bake for 10 minutes, or until puffed and golden. When completely cool, store in an airtight container.

PREPARATION TIME: 10 MINUTES   COOKING TIME: 10 MINUTES

Sun-dried tomato plaits

HERBED CHEESE TARTLETS

PASTRY
500 g (1 lb 2 oz/4 cups) plain (all-purpose) flour
1 teaspoon paprika
250 g (9 oz) butter, chopped
80 ml (2¹/₂ fl oz/¹/₃ cup) lemon juice
160–200 ml (5¹/₄–7 fl oz) iced water

FILLING
500 g (1 lb 2 oz) cottage cheese
2 tablespoons chopped chervil, plus extra, to garnish
2 tablespoons chopped tarragon
2 teaspoons snipped chives
125 ml (4 fl oz/¹/₂ cup) thick (double/heavy) cream
24 black olives, pitted and sliced

MAKES 48

To make the pastry, sift the flour, paprika and a pinch of salt into a large bowl. Add the butter and rub into the flour using your fingertips, until the mixture resembles fine breadcrumbs. Make a well in the centre and stir in the lemon juice and the iced water. Mix with a flat-bladed knife until the mixture comes together in beads. Gently gather together and lift out onto a lightly floured surface. Flatten into a disc, wrap in plastic wrap and refrigerate for 15 minutes.

Preheat the oven to 200°C (400°F/Gas 6). Grease two 12-hole round-based patty pans or mini muffin tins. Roll the dough out on a lightly floured surface to 3 mm (¹/₈ inch) thick and, using an 8 cm (3 inch) cutter, cut 24 rounds from the pastry and line the patty pans. Bake for 8–10 minutes, or until golden brown. Repeat with the remaining pastry.

To make the filling, beat together the cottage cheese, herbs and cream until smooth. Stir in the olives with some salt and black pepper. Spoon into the cases and garnish with chervil and black pepper.

PREPARATION TIME: 30 MINUTES +   COOKING TIME: 10 MINUTES

SMOKED TROUT PUFFS

1 sheet frozen puff pastry, thawed
1 egg, beaten
sesame seeds, for sprinkling
250 g (9 oz/1 cup) light cream cheese
2 tablespoons capers, rinsed, drained and finely chopped
2 spring onions (scallions), finely chopped
2 tablespoons chopped dill
320 g (11¼ oz) whole smoked trout, skinned, bones removed and flaked

Preheat the oven to 220°C (425°F/Gas 7). Lightly grease two baking trays. Cut 36 small squares from the sheet of puff pastry. Brush the tops lightly with the beaten egg and sprinkle with the sesame seeds.

Place on the baking trays and bake for about 8 minutes, or until puffed and well browned. Allow to cool, then gently split in half horizontally.

Soften the cream cheese and blend with the capers, spring onion and dill. Spread on the bases of the squares, top with some smoked trout, then replace the pastry tops at a slight angle.

MAKES 36   PREPARATION TIME: 25 MINUTES   COOKING TIME: 10 MINUTES

SPICY WON TON STRIPS

6 fresh won ton wrappers
oil, for frying
1 teaspoon Chinese five-spice
1 tablespoon sea salt, lightly crushed

MAKES 35

Cut the won ton wrappers into 1 cm (½ inch) strips with scissors.

Fill a deep heavy-based wok or frying pan one-third full of oil and heat to 180°C (350°F), or until a cube of bread dropped into the oil turns golden brown in 15 seconds. Deep-fry the won ton strips briefly in batches until golden brown, remove with a slotted spoon and drain on crumpled paper towels. While hot, sprinkle with a mixture of Chinese five-spice and sea salt. Allow to cool, then store in an airtight container.

PREPARATION TIME: 5 MINUTES   COOKING TIME: 10 MINUTES

Smoked trout puffs

MEXICAN LAYERED DIP

GUACAMOLE
3 ripe avocados
1 small tomato
1–2 red chillies, finely chopped
1 small red onion, finely chopped
1 tablespoon chopped coriander
(cilantro) leaves
1 tablespoon lime or lemon juice
2 tablespoons sour cream
1–2 drops habañero or Tabasco sauce

450 g (1 lb) tinned refried beans
35 g (1¼ oz) packet taco seasoning mix
300 g (10½ oz) sour cream
200 g (7 oz) ready-made salsa sauce
60 g (2¼ oz) cheddar cheese, grated
2 tablespoons chopped pitted black
olives
200 g (7 oz) corn chips
chopped coriander (cilantro) leaves,
to garnish

SERVES 12

To make the guacamole, roughly chop the avocado flesh. Put in a bowl and mash lightly with a fork. Cut the tomato in half horizontally and scoop out the seeds. Finely dice the flesh and add to the avocado. Stir in the chilli, onion, coriander, lime or lemon juice, sour cream and sauce. Season to taste. Cover and refrigerate until required.

Combine the refried beans and taco seasoning in a small bowl.

To assemble, spread the beans in the centre of a large platter or dish, leaving a border for the corn chips. Spoon the sour cream on top, leaving a small border of bean mixture showing. Repeat with the guacamole and salsa sauce so that you can see each layer. Sprinkle the top with cheese and olives.

Arrange some of the corn chips around the edge just before serving and garnish with the coriander. Serve with the remaining corn chips.

PREPARATION TIME: 1 HOUR   COOKING TIME: NIL

NOTES: Tabasco and habañero sauces are both made from fiery hot chillies, so taste before adding too much.
   This dip can be made 2 hours ahead, and refrigerated, covered.

THAI BEEF SALAD IN CUCUMBER CUPS

MARINADE
80 ml (2^1/$_2$ fl oz/^{1}/$_3$ cup) kecap manis
80 ml (2^1/$_2$ fl oz/^{1}/$_3$ cup) lime juice
1 red chilli, thinly sliced
1 tablespoon sesame oil

250 g (9 oz) beef eye fillet
7 Lebanese (short) cucumbers

SALAD
^{1}/$_2$ lemon grass stem, white part only,
finely chopped
60 ml (2 fl oz/^{1}/$_4$ cup) lime juice
1–2 red chillies, thinly sliced
20 g (^{3}/$_4$ oz) mint, finely chopped
20 g (^{3}/$_4$ oz) coriander (cilantro)
leaves, finely chopped
1 tablespoon fish sauce

MAKES 30

Combine the marinade ingredients in a bowl. Put the beef eye fillet in a non-metallic bowl, pour in the marinade and refrigerate for 2 hours, or overnight. Allow the meat to return to room temperature before cooking.

Heat a barbecue grill plate or chargrill pan and cook the beef. Cook for 7 minutes for medium, or until done to your liking. Allow to cool, then slice into thin strips. Combine the salad ingredients in a bowl and add the beef strips.

Cut off the ends of the cucumber and cut into 3 cm (1^1/$_4$ inch) thick slices. Using a melon baller, scoop out the flesh from each slice to make a 'cup' about 1 cm (^{1}/$_2$ inch) thick. Fill each cup with the Thai beef salad.

PREPARATION TIME: 25 MINUTES +   COOKING TIME: 10 MINUTES

NOTE: Prepare the salad and scooped out cucumber slices separately and refrigerate, then fill just before serving.

STUFFED ZUCCHINI

4 large zucchini (courgettes)
125 g (4^1/$_2$ oz) minced (ground) pork
60 g (2^1/$_4$ oz) raw prawns (shrimp), chopped
2 garlic cloves, crushed
2 tablespoons chopped coriander (cilantro)
leaves
^{1}/$_2$ teaspoon sugar
2 makrut (kaffir lime) leaves, chopped
2 red Asian shallots, finely chopped
60 ml (2 fl oz/^{1}/$_4$ cup) coconut cream
2 teaspoons fish sauce
1 tablespoon unsalted peanuts, chopped

MAKES ABOUT 24

Cut the zucchini into 4 cm (1^1/$_2$ inch) thick slices. Scoop out the centre with a melon baller, leaving 5 mm (^{1}/$_4$ inch) of flesh around the inside of the skin as well as on the bottom of each slice.

Combine the pork, prawn, garlic, coriander, sugar, makrut leaves, shallots, 2 tablespoons of the coconut cream and the fish sauce in a bowl. Spoon into the zucchini shells. Cover and refrigerate until close to serving time.

Put the zucchini shells in a bamboo or metal steamer over a saucepan of boiling water. Cover and steam for 10 minutes, or until the filling is cooked and zucchini tender. Serve dotted with coconut cream and sprinkled with the peanuts.

PREPARATION TIME: 30 MINUTES   COOKING TIME: 10 MINUTES

Thai beef salad in cucumber cups

OLIVE AND ALMOND PALMIERS

75 g (2½ oz) black olives, pitted and chopped
95 g (3¼ oz/1 cup) ground almonds
25 g (1 oz) parmesan cheese, grated
2 tablespoons chopped basil
60 ml (2 fl oz/¼ cup) olive oil
2 teaspoons wholegrain mustard
2 sheets frozen puff pastry, thawed
60 ml (2 fl oz/¼ cup) milk

MAKES ABOUT 24

Preheat the oven to 200°C (400°F/Gas 6). Line two baking trays with baking paper. In a food processor, process the olives, almonds, parmesan, basil, oil, mustard, ¼ teaspoon salt and ½ teaspoon cracked black pepper until they form a paste.

Lay out one sheet of pastry and cover evenly with half the olive-almond paste. Fold two opposite ends into the centre to meet.

Fold the same way again. Brush the pastry with the milk. Repeat the process with the remaining pastry and filling. Cut into 1.5 cm (⅝ inch) thick slices. Shape the slices into a V-shape, with the two sides curving out slightly. Place on the trays, leaving room for spreading. Bake for 15–20 minutes, or until puffed and golden. Allow to cool on a wire rack. Serve at room temperature.

PREPARATION TIME: 30 MINUTES   COOKING TIME: 20 MINUTES

NOTES: Palmiers can be cooked up to 6 hours ahead and stored in an airtight container.
    You can also use ready-made olive paste.

CORN AND RED CAPSICUM TARTLETS

3 sheets frozen puff pastry, thawed
310 g (11 oz) tinned corn kernels, drained
150 g (5½ oz) red leicester cheese, grated
1 small red capsicum (pepper), finely chopped
2 eggs, lightly beaten
60 ml (2 fl oz/¼ cup) buttermilk
170 ml (5½ fl oz/⅔ cup) thick (double/heavy) cream
1 teaspoon dijon mustard
dash Tabasco sauce
snipped chives, to garnish

MAKES ABOUT 36

Preheat the oven to 200°C (400°F/Gas 6). Lightly grease three 12-hole round-based patty pans or mini muffin tins. Using a 6 cm (2½ inch) round pastry cutter, cut circles from the pastry sheets. Press the circles into the prepared tins and prick the bases all over with a fork.

Combine the corn, cheese and capsicum in a bowl and season. Whisk the eggs, buttermilk, cream, mustard and Tabasco sauce in a measuring cup with a pouring lip. Spoon some of the vegetable mixture into the pastry cases, then pour the egg mixture over the top until the cases are almost full. Bake for 20–25 minutes, or until well risen and set. Serve cold. Garnish with snipped chives.

PREPARATION TIME: 20 MINUTES   COOKING TIME: 25 MINUTES

NOTE: The tarts can be made up to a day ahead and refrigerated, covered, in an airtight container, or frozen for up to 2 months.

SMOKED SALMON AND ROCKET ROLLS

200 g (7 oz) ricotta cheese
60 g (2¼ oz/¼ cup) crème fraîche or sour cream
2 teaspoons wasabi paste
1 tablespoon lime juice
12 slices brown bread, crusts removed
300 g (10½ oz) smoked salmon
100 g (3½ oz) baby rocket (arugula), trimmed
rocket (arugula) leaves, extra, to garnish

MAKES 36

Combine the ricotta, crème fraîche or sour cream, wasabi and lime juice in a bowl.

Roll the slices of bread out with a rolling pin to flatten.

Spread the ricotta over the bread, then top with the salmon and rocket, leaving a border. Roll up lengthways, wrap tightly in plastic wrap to hold the shape, then refrigerate for 30 minutes.

Unwrap, trim the ends and cut into 2 cm (³/₄ inch) slices. Garnish with rocket leaves.

PREPARATION TIME: 20 MINUTES +   COOKING TIME: NIL

Corn and red capsicum tartlets

VIETNAMESE LETTUCE-WRAPPED SPRING ROLLS

50 g (1³/₄ oz) dried mung bean vermicelli

2 tablespoons black fungus

20 rice paper wrappers

500 g (1 lb 2 oz) prawns (shrimp), peeled, deveined and finely chopped

150 g (5¹/₂ oz) minced (ground) pork

4 spring onions (scallions), chopped

45 g (1¹/₂ oz/¹/₂ cup) bean sprouts, trimmed, roughly chopped

1 teaspoon sugar

1 egg, beaten

oil, for deep-frying

20 lettuce leaves

90 g (3¹/₄ oz/1 cup) bean sprouts, extra, trimmed

1 large handful mint

VIETNAMESE DIPPING SAUCE

2 tablespoons fish sauce

2 tablespoons chopped coriander (cilantro) leaves

1 teaspoon chopped red chilli

1 teaspoon soft brown sugar

MAKES 20

Put the vermicelli and fungus in separate heatproof bowls. Cover with hot water and soak for 10 minutes, or until soft. Drain both, and chop the fungus roughly.

Using a pastry brush, brush both sides of each rice paper wrapper liberally with water. Allow to stand for 2 minutes, or until they become soft and pliable. Stack the wrappers on a plate. Sprinkle over a little extra water and cover the plate with plastic wrap to keep the wrappers moist until needed.

Combine the vermicelli, fungus, prawn meat, pork, spring onion, bean sprouts, sugar and salt and pepper in a bowl.

Put 1 tablespoon of the filling along the base of a wrapper. Fold in the sides, roll the wrapper up tightly, and brush the seam with the egg. Repeat with the remaining wrappers and filling.

Press the rolls with paper towels to remove any excess water. Heat 4–5 cm (1¹/₂–2 inches) oil in a wok or deep frying pan to 180°C (350°F), or until a cube of bread browns in 15 seconds. Add the spring rolls in batches and cook for 2–3 minutes, or until dark golden brown. Drain on paper towels.

Put a spring roll in each lettuce leaf, top with 1 tablespoon bean sprouts and two mint leaves, and roll up to form a neat parcel. Serve with the dipping sauce.

To make the Vietnamese dipping sauce, combine all the ingredients in a bowl and add 2 tablespoons cold water. Mix well.

PREPARATION TIME: 50 MINUTES +   COOKING TIME: 20 MINUTES

SCALLOP FRITTERS

250 g (9 oz) scallops
6 eggs
25 g (1 oz) parmesan cheese, grated
3 garlic cloves, crushed
125 g (4½ oz/1 cup) plain (all-purpose) flour
2 tablespoons chopped thyme
2 tablespoons chopped oregano
oil, for pan-frying
whole-egg mayonnaise, to serve

MAKES 40

Clean and roughly chop the scallops. Lightly beat the eggs and combine with the parmesan, garlic, flour and herbs. Stir in the scallops.

Heat 3 cm (1¼ inches) oil in a deep frying pan to 180°C (350°F), or until a cube of bread dropped into the oil turns golden brown in 15 seconds. Cook the fritters in batches. Using 1 tablespoon of batter for each fritter, pour into the oil and cook for 4–5 minutes, until golden brown. Drain on crumpled paper towels and sprinkle lightly with salt. Serve with mayonnaise for dipping.

PREPARATION TIME: 20 MINUTES   COOKING TIME: 20 MINUTES +

CHEESE FRITTERS

175 g (6 oz) block firm feta cheese
125 g (4½ oz) mozzarella cheese
40 g (1½ oz/⅓ cup) plain (all-purpose) flour
1 egg, beaten
50 g (1¾ oz/½ cup) dry breadcrumbs
oil, for pan-frying

MAKES ABOUT 35–40

Cut the feta and mozzarella into 2 cm (¾ inch) cubes. Combine the flour and ¼ teaspoon black pepper on a sheet of baking paper. Toss the cheese lightly in the seasoned flour and shake off the excess.

Dip the cheese into the egg a few pieces at a time. Coat with the breadcrumbs and shake off the excess. Repeat the process with the remaining cheese and crumbs. Arrange on a foil-lined baking tray and refrigerate, covered, for 25 minutes.

Heat 3 cm (1¼ inches) oil in a deep frying pan to 180°C (350°F), or until a cube of bread dropped into the oil turns golden brown in 15 seconds in 15 seconds. Cook a few pieces of cheese at a time over medium heat, for 2–3 minutes each batch, or until golden and crisp. Drain on crumpled paper towels.

PREPARATION TIME: 15 MINUTES +   COOKING TIME: 30 MINUTES +

NOTE: Serve with sweet chilli, plum or cranberry sauce.

SESAME SHAPES

185 g (6½ oz/1½ cups) self-raising flour
50 g (1¾ oz/⅓ cup) sesame seeds, toasted
2 teaspoons finely grated orange zest
2 eggs
2 teaspoons sesame oil
250 ml (9 fl oz/1 cup) milk
80 ml (2½ fl oz/⅓ cup) orange juice
butter or oil, for greasing
125 g (4½ oz) sun-dried tomatoes, finely chopped

FILLING
200 g (7 oz) cream cheese
2 tablespoons chopped coriander (cilantro) leaves

MAKES ABOUT 30

Sift the flour and a pinch of salt into a bowl, stir in the sesame seeds and orange zest and make a well in the centre. With a fork, gradually whisk in the combined egg, sesame oil, milk and orange juice to make a smooth lump-free batter. Set aside for 15 minutes.

Heat a frying pan and brush lightly with melted butter or oil. Pour 80 ml (2½ fl oz/⅓ cup) batter into the pan and cook over medium heat for 3–4 minutes, or until bubbles appear on the surface. Turn over and cook the other side. Transfer to a plate and cover with a tea towel (dish towel) while cooking the remaining batter.

Use biscuit (cookie) cutters to cut out various shapes (you will be sandwiching three of each shape together so make sure you have the right number of each).

To make the filling, mix the cream cheese and coriander and use to sandwich together three shapes. Decorate with sun-dried tomato.

PREPARATION TIME: 35 MINUTES +   COOKING TIME: 20 MINUTES

NOTE: These can be joined and cut into shapes a day ahead. Store in an airtight container in the refrigerator.

TURKEY AND BRIE TRIANGLES

8 slices white bread
100 g (3½ oz) cranberry sauce
120 g (4 oz) sliced turkey breast
120 g (4 oz) brie, sliced
4 butter lettuce leaves

MAKES 16

Trim the crusts from the bread. Spread the slices with cranberry sauce. Add the turkey breast, brie and lettuce leaves and make into sandwiches. Cut into four triangles to serve.

PREPARATION TIME: 10 MINUTES   COOKING TIME: NIL

CHICKEN, ROCKET AND WALNUT SANDWICHES

2 tablespoons oil
250 g (9 oz) boneless, skinless chicken breast
500 g (1 lb 2 oz) boneless, skinless chicken thigh
250 g (9 oz/1 cup) whole-egg mayonnaise
100 g (3½ oz) celery, finely chopped
90 g (3¼ oz/¾ cup) chopped walnuts
20 slices bread
1 large handful rocket (arugula)

MAKES 30

Heat the oil in a frying pan over medium heat and cook the chicken breast and thigh until lightly browned. Allow to cool, then chop finely.

Combine the chicken with the mayonnaise, celery and walnuts. Season to taste.

Make sandwiches using the chicken mixture and add the rocket to each. Remove the crusts and cut each sandwich into three fingers.

PREPARATION TIME: 15 MINUTES +   COOKING TIME: 15 MINUTES

Turkey and brie triangles

MINI QUICHE LORRAINES

3 sheets frozen shortcrust (pie) pastry, thawed
60 g (2¼ oz) gruyère cheese, grated
30 g (1 oz) butter
2 bacon slices, finely chopped
1 onion, finely chopped
2 eggs
185 ml (6 fl oz/¾ cup) pouring (whipping) cream
½ teaspoon freshly grated nutmeg
chives, cut into short strips

MAKES 24

Preheat the oven to 190°C (375°F/Gas 5). Lightly grease two 12-hole round-based patty pans or mini muffin tins. Using a plain 8 cm (3 inch) cutter, cut rounds of pastry and fit in the tins. Divide the cheese evenly among the pastry bases. Cover and refrigerate while making the filling.

Heat the butter in a small frying pan and cook the bacon and onion for 2–3 minutes, or until tender. Drain on paper towels. When cool, divide the mixture evenly among the bases. Whisk the eggs in a bowl with the cream, nutmeg and a little freshly ground black pepper. Pour or spoon carefully over the bacon mixture.

Put a few strips of chive on top of each quiche to decorate. Bake for 20 minutes, or until lightly browned and set. Serve at room temperature.

PREPARATION TIME: 20 MINUTES +   COOKING TIME: 25 MINUTES

NOTE: These quiches can be cooked up to 2 days ahead and stored in an airtight container in the refrigerator. They can be frozen in single layers for up to 2 months. Reheat in a 180°C (350°F/Gas 4) oven.

PAN BAGNAT

4 crusty bread rolls, or 1 baguette, sliced into 4 chunks
1 garlic clove
60 ml (2 fl oz/¼ cup) olive oil
1 tablespoon red wine vinegar
3 tablespoons torn basil
2 tomatoes, sliced
2 hard-boiled eggs, sliced
75 g (2½ oz) tinned tuna
8 anchovy fillets
1 Lebanese (short) cucumber, sliced
½ green capsicum (pepper), thinly sliced
1 French shallot, thinly sliced

SERVES 4

Slice the bread rolls or baguette chunks in half and remove some of the soft centre from the tops. Cut the garlic clove in half and rub the insides of the bread with the cut sides. Sprinkle both sides of the bread with olive oil, vinegar, and salt and pepper.

Put the remaining ingredients on the base of the rolls, cover with the other half and wrap each sandwich in foil. Press firmly with a light weight and stand in a cool place for 1 hour before serving.

PREPARATION TIME: 15 MINUTES +   COOKING TIME: NIL

BACON AND MUSHROOM CREAM BITES

1 egg yolk, lightly beaten
2 sheets frozen shortcrust (pie) pastry, thawed
2 tablespoons oil
375 g (12 oz) mushrooms, finely chopped
4 bacon slices, finely chopped
4 spring onions (scallions), finely chopped
15 g (½ oz) flat-leaf (Italian) parsley, finely chopped
250 g (9 oz) cream cheese, softened
4 eggs

MAKES 18

Preheat the oven to 210°C (415°F/Gas 6–7). Lightly grease a shallow 23 cm (9 inch) square cake tin. Brush egg yolk over one sheet of pastry. Put the other sheet over the top and gently press together. Trim the edges to fit the tin. Prick the pastry evenly with a fork and bake for 15 minutes, or until golden brown. Reduce the oven to 180°C (350°F/Gas 4).

Heat the oil in a heavy-based frying pan. Add the mushrooms and stir over medium heat for 5 minutes, or until well browned. Remove from the heat and stir in the bacon, spring onion and parsley. Season to taste. Allow to cool.

Beat the cream cheese and eggs in a small bowl using electric beaters for 5 minutes. Add the cooled mushroom mixture and stir to combine. Pour the mixture onto the cooked pastry base. Bake for 25 minutes, or until firm and lightly browned. Allow to cool in the tin. Cut into triangles to serve.

PREPARATION TIME: 15 MINUTES +   COOKING TIME: 45 MINUTES ·

MINI SCONES WITH HAM, LEEK AND PORT FIGS

250 g (9 oz/2 cups) plain (all-purpose) flour
3 teaspoons baking powder
110 g (3³/₄ oz) butter
100 g (3¹/₂ oz) stilton cheese
2 tablespoons snipped chives
185 ml (6 fl oz/³/₄ cup) milk

FILLING
250 ml (9 fl oz/1 cup) port
6 large dried figs, stems removed
1 teaspoon sugar
1 large leek
1 teaspoon dijon mustard
2 teaspoons red wine vinegar
1 tablespoon olive oil
150 g (5¹/₂ oz) shaved ham

MAKES ABOUT 40

Sift the flour, baking powder and ³/₄ teaspoon salt into a large bowl. Coarsely grate the butter and cheese into the flour and rub in using your fingertips until the pieces are the size of coarse breadcrumbs. Stir in the chives. Pour in the milk and combine with a fork until large clumps form. Turn onto a floured surface and press into a ball.

Preheat the oven to 220°C (425°F/Gas 7). Roll the dough out on a floured surface into a 15 x 25 cm (6 x 10 inch) rectangle. With the long edge of the dough facing you, fold in both ends so they meet in the centre, then fold the dough in half widthways. Roll again into a 15 x 25 cm (6 x 10 inch) rectangle, about 1 cm (¹/₂ inch) thick. Cut rounds close together with a 3 cm (1¹/₄ inch) cutter. Push the scraps together and roll and cut as before. Place 2.5 cm (1 inch) apart on a baking tray and refrigerate for 20 minutes. Bake for 10–12 minutes, or until lightly browned.

In a small saucepan, heat the port, figs and sugar. Bring to the boil, reduce the heat and simmer for 15 minutes. Remove the figs and, when cooled, roughly chop. Simmer the liquid for about 3 minutes, until reduced and syrupy. Put the figs back in and stir to combine. Set aside.

Discard any tough leaves from the leek, then rinse the leek. Trim off the dark green tops. Slit the leek lengthways, almost to the bottom, roll a quarter, turn and slit again. Wash well, drain and steam for about 10 minutes, or until very soft. Roughly chop, then combine with the mustard, vinegar and oil. Season.

Cut the scones in half. Put a folded piece of ham on each bottom half, top with a teaspoon each of leek and fig mixture, then replace the tops.

PREPARATION TIME: 40 MINUTES +   COOKING TIME: 45 MINUTES

BOREK

400 g (14 oz) feta cheese
2 eggs, beaten
2 large handfuls flat-leaf
(Italian) parsley, chopped
375 g (13 oz) filo pastry
80 ml (2½ fl oz/⅓ cup) olive oil

MAKES 24

Preheat the oven to 180°C (350°F/Gas 4). Lightly grease a baking tray. Crumble the feta into a large bowl using your fingers. Mix in the eggs and parsley and season with freshly ground black pepper.

Cover the filo pastry with a damp tea towel (dish towel) so it doesn't dry out. Remove one sheet at a time. Brushing each sheet lightly with olive oil, layer four sheets on top of one another. Cut the pastry into four 7 cm (2¾ inch) strips.

Put 2 rounded teaspoons of the feta mixture in one corner of each strip and fold diagonally, creating a triangle pillow. Put on the baking tray, seam side down, and brush with olive oil. Repeat with the remaining pastry and filling to make 24 parcels. Bake for 20 minutes, or until golden.

PREPARATION TIME: 1 HOUR   COOKING TIME: 20 MINUTES

MINI LENTIL BURGERS WITH TOMATO RELISH

185 g (6½ oz/1 cup) brown lentils
1 bay leaf
1 onion, roughly chopped
1 garlic clove, crushed
1 small leek, thinly sliced
1 small carrot, finely grated
80 g (2¾ oz/1 cup) fresh breadcrumbs
2 egg yolks
2 tablespoons chopped coriander
(cilantro) leaves
2 tablespoons oil
8 slices bread, cut into 4 cm
(1½ inch) squares
ready-made tomato relish, to serve

MAKES 32

Place the lentils and bay leaf in a saucepan and cover with plenty of water. Bring to the boil and simmer for 20–30 minutes, or until tender. Drain well and discard the bay leaf.

Combine half the cooked lentils with the onion and garlic in a food processor until the mixture forms a smooth paste. Transfer to a bowl and mix with the remaining lentils, leek, carrot, breadcrumbs, egg yolks and coriander. Season. Form level tablespoons of the mixture into mini patties.

Heat some of the oil in a non-stick frying pan and cook the mini patties in batches until browned on both sides, adding more oil as necessary. Drain on paper towels and serve warm, on the bread squares, with a dollop of tomato relish on top.

PREPARATION TIME: 40 MINUTES   COOKING TIME: 55 MINUTES

TAMALE BEEF AND BEAN PIES

1 tablespoon oil
1 small onion, finely chopped
250 g (9 oz) minced (ground) beef
1 garlic clove, crushed
1/4 teaspoon chilli powder
200 g (7 oz) tinned crushed tomatoes
375 ml (13 fl oz/1½ cups) beef stock
300 g (10½ oz) tinned red kidney beans, drained
360 g (12¾ oz/2½ cups) masa harina
1 teaspoon baking powder
125 g (4½ oz) butter, chilled and chopped
125 g (4½ oz) cheddar cheese, grated
sour cream, to serve

MAKES 30

To make the filling, heat the oil in a frying pan over medium heat. Add the onion and cook over low heat for 3–4 minutes, or until soft. Increase the heat, add the beef and cook until browned all over. Add the garlic, chilli, tomato and 125 ml (4 fl oz/½ cup) of the stock. Bring to the boil, then reduce the heat and simmer for 35 minutes, or until the liquid has evaporated to a thick sauce. Stir in the beans and cool.

Lightly grease 30 holes in deep mini muffin tins. Sift the masa harina, baking powder and ½ teaspoon salt into a bowl. Rub the butter into the flour with your fingertips until it resembles fine breadcrumbs. Make a well in the centre and, with a flat-bladed knife, mix in the remaining stock, then use your hands to bring the mixture together into a ball. Divide into thirds and roll two-thirds between two sheets of baking paper. Cut out rounds with a 7 cm (2¾ inch) cutter and line the muffin holes. Trim the edges and reserve any leftover pastry.

Preheat the oven to 200°C (400°F/Gas 6). Spoon the filling into the pastry cases and sprinkle with the cheddar. Roll out the remaining pastry and reserved pastry as above. Cut into 4 cm (1½ inch) rounds to cover the tops of the pies. Brush the edges with water and place over the filling. Trim the edges and press the pastry together to seal. Bake for 20–25 minutes, or until the pastry is crisp and lightly browned. Serve with sour cream.

PREPARATION TIME: 1 HOUR   COOKING TIME: 1 HOUR 5 MINUTES

NOTE: Masa harina is a type of white flour made from maize.

SAUSAGE ROLLS

3 sheets frozen puff pastry, thawed
2 eggs, beaten
750 g (1 lb 10 oz) minced (ground) sausage meat
1 onion, finely chopped
1 garlic clove, crushed
80 g (2¾ oz/1 cup) fresh breadcrumbs
3 tablespoons chopped flat-leaf (Italian) parsley
3 tablespoons chopped thyme
½ teaspoon ground sage
½ teaspoon freshly grated nutmeg
½ teaspoon ground cloves

MAKES 36

Preheat the oven to 200°C (400°F/Gas 6). Lightly grease two baking trays. Cut the pastry sheets in half and lightly brush the edges with some of the beaten egg.

Mix half the remaining egg with the remaining ingredients in a large bowl, then divide into six even portions. Pipe or spoon the filling down the centre of each piece of pastry, then brush the edges with some of the egg. Fold the pastry over the filling, overlapping the edges and placing the join underneath. Brush the rolls with more egg, then cut each into six short pieces.

Cut two small slashes on top of each roll and put on the baking trays. Bake for 15 minutes, then reduce the oven temperature to 180°C (350°F/Gas 4) and bake for a further 15 minutes, or until puffed and golden.

PREPARATION TIME: 30 MINUTES   COOKING TIME: 30 MINUTES

SPICY SAUSAGE ROLL-UPS

2 sheets shortcrust (pie) pastry
2 tablespoons dijon mustard
5 sticks cabanossi
1 egg yolk, beaten

MAKES ABOUT 25

Preheat the oven to 200°C (400°F/Gas 6). Cut each pastry sheet in half. Cut triangles with bases of 6 cm (2½ inches). Put a small dob of mustard at the base of each pastry piece. Cut the cabanossi into 7 cm (2¾ inch) lengths and place across the mustard on the pastry triangles.

Dampen the tips of the triangles with a little water. Working from the base, roll each pastry triangle around the pieces of cabanossi. Press lightly to secure the tip to the rest of the pastry.

Put the roll-ups on a lightly greased baking tray and brush with a mixture of egg yolk and 2 teaspoons cold water. Bake for 15–20 minutes, or until golden brown.

PREPARATION TIME: 20 MINUTES   COOKING TIME: 20 MINUTES

NOTE: These can be made up to 2 days ahead, refrigerated, then gently reheated in the oven when required.

Sausage rolls

SAVOURY POTATO EMPANADAS

60 ml (2 fl oz/¹/₄ cup) olive oil
1 small onion, finely diced
2 spring onions (scallions), thinly sliced
1 garlic clove, crushed
100 g (3¹/₂ oz) minced (ground) beef
1 teaspoon ground cumin
1 teaspoon dried oregano
125 g (4¹/₂ oz) all-purpose potatoes, cubed
4 sheets frozen puff pastry, thawed
50 g (1³/₄ oz) black olives, pitted and quartered
1 hard-boiled egg, finely chopped
1 egg, separated
pinch paprika
pinch sugar

MAKES 32

In a heavy-based frying pan, heat 1 tablespoon of the oil, add the onion and spring onion and stir for 5 minutes. Stir in the garlic and cook for 3 minutes. Remove from the pan and set aside.

Heat another tablespoon of oil in the pan, add the beef and stir over medium heat until browned, breaking up any lumps with a fork. Add the onion mixture and stir well.

Add the cumin, oregano, and ¹/₂ teaspoon each of salt and black pepper, and stir for a further 2 minutes. Transfer to a bowl and cool. Wipe out the pan with paper towel.

Heat another tablespoon of oil in the pan, add the potato and stir over high heat for 1 minute. Reduce the heat to low and stir for 5 minutes, or until tender. Cool slightly and then gently mix into the beef mixture.

Preheat the oven to 200°C (400°F/Gas 6). Cut rounds from the pastry with an 8 cm (3 inch) cutter. Lightly grease two baking trays.

Spoon heaped teaspoons of the beef mixture onto one side of each pastry round, leaving a border wide enough for the pastry to be folded over. Put a few olive quarters and some chopped egg on top of the beef mixture. Brush the border with egg white. Carefully fold the pastry over to make a half moon shape, pressing firmly to seal. Press the edges with a floured fork, to decorate, and then gently transfer to the baking trays. Stir the egg yolk, paprika and sugar together and brush over the empanadas. Bake for 15 minutes, or until golden brown and puffed.

PREPARATION TIME: 1 HOUR   COOKING TIME: 40 MINUTES

NOTE: The puffs can be made 2 days ahead or frozen for 2 months.

SPICY KOFTAS

500 g (1 lb 2 oz) minced (ground) lamb
1 small onion, finely chopped
1 garlic clove, crushed
1 teaspoon ground coriander
1 teaspoon ground cumin
1/4 teaspoon ground cinnamon
1/2 teaspoon finely chopped red chilli
1 teaspoon tomato paste (concentrated purée)
1 tablespoon chopped mint
1 tablespoon chopped coriander (cilantro) leaves
oil, for frying

YOGHURT DIP
1 tomato, peeled, seeded and chopped
1/2 Lebanese (short) cucumber, chopped
1 garlic clove, crushed
1 tablespoon chopped mint
125 g (4 1/2 oz/1/2 cup) plain yoghurt

MAKES 45

Combine the lamb, onion, garlic, coriander, cumin, cinnamon, chilli, tomato paste and mint and coriander leaves in a large bowl and mix well using your hands. Season well, then roll into small balls (about 1 1/2 teaspoons each).

Heat a little oil in a large heavy-based frying pan over high heat. Cook the koftas in batches until well browned all over and cooked through. Drain on crumpled paper towels.

Combine the dip ingredients in a small bowl and mix well.

Skewer each kofta with a cocktail stick and serve with the dip.

PREPARATION TIME: 25 MINUTES   COOKING TIME: 25 MINUTES

NOTES: You can freeze the cooked koftas. When required, thaw, cover with foil and reheat in an ovenproof dish in a 180°C (350°F/Gas 4) oven for 5–10 minutes.
    The dip can be made several hours ahead.

CHILLI BEEF QUESADILLAS

1 1/2 tablespoons oil
1 onion, chopped
2 garlic cloves, crushed
400 g (14 oz) minced (ground) beef
325 g (11 oz) ready-made Mexican black bean salsa
6 flour tortillas
125 g (4 1/2 oz) grated cheddar cheese

MAKES ABOUT 36

Heat 1 tablespoon of the oil in a frying pan and cook the onion and garlic for 2–3 minutes. Add the beef and cook for 5–7 minutes, or until brown, breaking up any lumps. Stir in the salsa. Bring to the boil, reduce the heat and simmer for 3–4 minutes, or until the mixture reduces and thickens. Season.

Put three of the tortillas on a work surface and sprinkle with the cheddar. Spoon the beef evenly over the cheese, then top with another three tortillas. Heat the remaining oil in a 25 cm (10 inch) frying pan and cook the stacks for 3–4 minutes each side, or until golden brown. Remove from the pan, trim off the sides and cut into 5 cm (2 inch) squares.

PREPARATION TIME: 15 MINUTES   COOKING TIME: 25 MINUTES

Spicy koftas

SPINACH PIE DIAMONDS

250 g (9 oz/2 cups) plain (all-purpose) flour
30 g (1 oz) butter, chopped
60 ml (2 fl oz/¼ cup) olive oil
125 ml (4 fl oz/½ cup) warm water
olive oil, extra, for brushing

FILLING
420 g (15 oz) English spinach
1 leek, white part only, halved lengthways and thinly sliced
¼ teaspoon freshly grated nutmeg
2 teaspoons chopped dill
200 g (7 oz) feta cheese, crumbled
1 tablespoon dry breadcrumbs
3 eggs, lightly beaten
2 tablespoons olive oil

MAKES ABOUT 15

Lightly grease a 3 cm (1¼ inch) deep baking tin with a base measuring 17 x 26 cm (6½ x 10½ inches).

Sift the flour and ½ teaspoon salt into a bowl. Rub the butter into the flour until it resembles fine breadcrumbs. Pour in the oil and rub it in by lifting the flour mixture onto one hand and lightly rubbing the other hand over the top. The mixture should clump together. Make a well in the centre and, while mixing by hand, add enough water to form a firm supple dough. Knead gently to bring the dough together — it may not be completely smooth. Cover with plastic wrap and chill for 1 hour.

Trim away the bottom quarter from the spinach stalks. Wash and shred the remaining leaves and stalks. Pile the spinach onto a tea towel (dish towel), twist tightly and squeeze out as much moisture as possible. Put into a bowl with the leek, nutmeg, dill, feta, breadcrumbs and ½ teaspoon cracked black pepper.

Preheat the oven to 220°C (425°F/Gas 7). Roll out just over half the dough on a lightly floured surface until large enough to line the base and sides of the tin. Lift the dough into the tin, pressing evenly over the base and sides.

Add the eggs and oil to the spinach mixture. Mix with your hand, but do not overmix. Spoon into the pastry-lined tin.

Roll out the remaining pastry on a lightly floured surface until large enough to cover the tin. Lift onto the tin and press the two pastry edges firmly together to seal. Trim the excess pastry with a sharp knife from the outer edge of the tin, then brush the top with a little extra olive oil. Using a sharp knife, mark into three strips lengthways and then diagonally into diamonds. Make two or three small slits through the top layer of pastry to allow the steam to escape during cooking.

Bake the pie on the centre shelf for 45–50 minutes, or until well browned. Cover with foil if the pastry is overbrowning. The pie is cooked if it slides when you gently shake the tin. Turn out onto a wire rack to cool for 10 minutes, then transfer to a cutting board or back into the tin to cut into diamonds.

PREPARATION TIME: 50 MINUTES +   COOKING TIME: 50 MINUTES

MINI CROISSANTS

40 g (1½ oz) butter
3 onions, finely chopped
12 pitted black olives, thinly sliced
2 tablespoons chopped flat-leaf (Italian) parsley
3 sheets frozen puff pastry, thawed
1 egg, beaten

MAKES 30

Melt the butter in a frying pan and cook the onion over medium–low heat for 20 minutes, or until golden. Remove from the heat and stir in the olives, parsley, and salt and cracked black pepper. Allow to cool. Lightly grease a baking tray.

Cut each sheet of pastry in half, then each half into five triangles with a base (shortest side) of 8 cm (3 inches). You will have a couple of odd shapes left at each end. Put a little onion mixture at the base of each triangle and roll up towards the point, enclosing the filling. Curl the ends around to form a croissant shape.

Put the croissants on the baking tray and refrigerate for 30 minutes. Preheat the oven to 200°C (400°F/Gas 6). Brush each croissant with beaten egg. Bake for 20 minutes, or until puffed and golden.

PREPARATION TIME: 30 MINUTES +   COOKING TIME: 40 MINUTES

CORN MINI MUFFINS WITH PRAWNS AND DILL MAYO

250 g (9 oz/2 cups) plain (all-purpose) flour, sifted
110 g (3½ oz/¾ cup) cornmeal
1 tablespoon baking powder
55 g (2 oz/¼ cup) sugar
2 eggs, beaten
125 g (4½ oz) butter, melted
250 ml (9 fl oz/1 cup) milk
3 tablespoons finely chopped dill
1 tablespoon lemon juice
1 teaspoon horseradish cream
375 g (12 oz/1½ cups) whole-egg mayonnaise
300 g (10½ oz) small cooked prawns (shrimp)

MAKES ABOUT 50

Preheat the oven to 200°C (400°F/Gas 6). Lightly grease two 12-hole mini muffin tins. Sift the flour into a large bowl and mix with the cornmeal, baking powder, sugar and ½ teaspoon salt. Add the eggs, butter and milk. Stir until just combined. Spoon small amounts into the muffin tins, filling the holes three-quarters full. Cook for 15–20 minutes, or until lightly browned. Turn onto a wire rack to cool. Repeat until you have used all the mixture.

Mix the dill, lemon juice and horseradish cream into the mayonnaise and add plenty of salt and black pepper.

When the muffins are cool, scoop out a small piece from the top, as you would with a butterfly cake, and spoon a little dill mayonnaise into the cavity. Top with a prawn and some freshly ground black pepper.

PREPARATION TIME: 15 MINUTES   COOKING TIME: 40 MINUTES

Mini croissants

DOLMADES

200 g (7 oz) vine leaves in brine
250 g (9 oz/1 cup) medium-grain white
rice
1 small onion, finely chopped
1 tablespoon olive oil
60 g (2¼ oz) pine nuts, toasted
2 tablespoons currants
2 tablespoons chopped dill
1 tablespoon finely chopped mint
1 tablespoon finely chopped flat-leaf
(Italian) parsley
80 ml (2½ fl oz/⅓ cup) olive oil, extra
2 tablespoons lemon juice
500 ml (17 fl oz/2 cups) chicken stock

EGG AND LEMON SAUCE
375 ml (12 fl oz/1½ cups) chicken stock
1 tablespoon cornflour (cornstarch)
3 eggs
2–3 tablespoons lemon juice

MAKES 24

Soak the vine leaves in cold water for 15 minutes, then remove and pat dry. Cut off any stems. Reserve some leaves to line the saucepan and discard any that have holes or look poor. Meanwhile, soak the rice in boiling water for 10 minutes to soften, then drain.

To make the filling, put the rice, onion, olive oil, pine nuts, currants, herbs and salt and pepper, to taste, in a large bowl and mix well.

Lay some leaves, vein side down, on a flat surface. Put 1 tablespoon of filling in the centre of each, fold the stalk end over the filling, then the left and right sides into the centre, and finally roll firmly towards the tip. The dolmades should resemble a small cigar. Repeat with the remaining filling and leaves.

Use the reserved vine leaves to line the base of a large, heavy-based saucepan. Drizzle with 1 tablespoon of the extra olive oil. Add the dolmades, packing them tightly in one layer, then pour the remaining oil and the lemon juice over them.

Pour the stock over the dolmades and cover with an inverted plate to stop the dolmades moving around while cooking. Bring to the boil, then reduce the heat and simmer, covered, for 45 minutes. Remove with a slotted spoon. Serve warm or cold. These can be served with lemon wedges.

Meanwhile, to make the sauce, bring the chicken stock to the boil in a saucepan. Mix the cornflour with enough cold water to make a paste. Add to the stock and stir until the mixture thickens. Simmer for 2–3 minutes, then remove from the heat and cool slightly. Separate the eggs and beat the whites in a large bowl until stiff peaks form. Add the yolks and beat until light and fluffy. Mix in the lemon juice. Gradually pour in the thickened stock, beating constantly. Return the sauce to the pan and cook over low heat, stirring constantly for 1–2 minutes. Season, to taste, remove from the heat and stir for 1 minute. Serve with the dolmades.

PREPARATION TIME: 40 MINUTES + COOKING TIME: 45 MINUTES

NOTE: Unused vine leaves can be stored in brine in an airtight container in the fridge for up to 1 week.

GOAT'S CHEESE TARTLETS

250 g (9 oz/2 cups) plain (all-purpose)
flour
150 g (5¹/₂ oz) butter, chilled and chopped
2 tablespoons milk

FILLING
12 sun-dried tomatoes, sliced
200 g (7 oz) goat's cheese, chopped
2 tablespoons chopped basil
20–30 black olives, pitted and sliced
2 tablespoons chopped spring onion
(scallion) tops
4 eggs, beaten
250 ml (9 fl oz/1 cup) pouring (whipping)
cream

MAKES 30

Sift the flour and a pinch of salt into a bowl. Add the butter and rub it in until the mixture resembles fine breadcrumbs. Make a well and add enough milk to mix to a soft dough, using a knife. Lift onto a floured surface and gather into a ball. Chill in plastic wrap for 30 minutes.

Preheat the oven to 180°C (350°F/Gas 4). Lightly grease two 12-hole round-based patty pans or mini muffin tins. Roll out the pastry to 2 mm (¹/₈ inch) and cut 30 rounds with an 8 cm (3 inch) cutter. Line the bases and prick the pastry lightly. Bake for 7 minutes, or until cooked but not coloured.

Arrange the sun-dried tomatoes in the bases and cover with the cheese, basil, olives and spring onion. Combine the eggs and cream in a small bowl and season. Spoon the mixture over the filling and bake, for 15 minutes, or until the filling is just set. Repeat with the remaining pastry and filling. Serve at room temperature.

PREPARATION TIME: 40 MINUTES +   COOKING TIME: 25 MINUTES

SMOKED TROUT TARTLETS

1 loaf sliced white bread, crusts removed
60 g (2¹/₄ oz) butter, melted
1 smoked trout (about 300 g/10¹/₂ oz),
skinned, bones removed and flaked
1 tablespoon snipped chives
60 g (2¹/₄ oz/¹/₄ cup) whole-egg
mayonnaise
2 spring onions (scallions), finely chopped
1 teaspoon horseradish cream
1 teaspoon wholegrain mustard
black olives, pitted and cut into strips,
to garnish

MAKES 34

Preheat the oven to 120°C (250°F/Gas ¹/₂). Flatten the bread slices with a rolling pin. Cut 8 cm (3 inch) rounds with a cutter, then brush both sides with butter. Press into two 12-hole round-based patty pans or mini muffin tins. Bake for 10 minutes, or until crisp. Cool. Repeat to use all the bread.

Put the trout in a bowl and add the chives, mayonnaise, spring onion, horseradish cream and mustard. Season and mix well.

Spoon the filling into the tartlet cases, then garnish with strips of olives.

PREPARATION TIME: 40 MINUTES +   COOKING TIME: 20 MINUTES

NOTE: The bread cases can be made 2 days ahead and stored in an airtight container.

Goat's cheese tartlets

PORK SAN CHOY BAU

1 tablespoon oil
400 g (14 oz) minced (ground) pork
230 g (8¹/₂ oz) tinned water chestnuts, drained and finely chopped
125 g (4¹/₂ oz) tinned bamboo shoots, drained and finely chopped
6 spring onions (scallions), finely chopped
2 tablespoons dry sherry
1 tablespoon soy sauce
2 teaspoons sesame oil
2 teaspoons oyster sauce
tiny lettuce leaves, such as cos (romaine), iceberg or witlof (chicory/Belgian endive)
chopped mint, to serve

SAUCE
2 tablespoons plum sauce
1 tablepoon hoisin sauce
1 teaspoon soy sauce

MAKES 25

Heat the oil in a frying pan or wok, add the pork and cook, stirring, over high heat until brown all over. Break up any lumps of pork with the back of a fork. Add the water chestnuts, bamboo shoots and spring onion. Toss well and cook for 1 minute.

Combine the sherry, soy sauce, sesame oil and oyster sauce. Add to the wok, toss well and cook for 2 minutes. Remove from the heat.

To make the dipping sauce, combine all the ingredients in a bowl with 2 tablespoons water.

To serve, put about 1 tablespoon of warm pork mixture on each lettuce leaf. Sprinkle with the chopped mint. Drizzle the sauce over the top.

PREPARATION TIME: 25 MINUTES   COOKING TIME: 10 MINUTES

NOTE: The pork can be prepared early in the day and refrigerated. Reheat to serve. The dipping sauce can be mixed the day before and refrigerated.

BABY SQUASH WITH RICE STUFFING

24 baby (pattypan) yellow squash
1 tablespoon oil
2 teaspoons Thai red curry paste
1 spring onion (scallion), finely chopped
1 small red capsicum (pepper), finely chopped
185 g (6½ oz/1 cup) cooked jasmine rice
1 tablespoon finely chopped coriander (cilantro) leaves
2 makrut (kaffir lime) leaves, finely shredded
coriander (cilantro) leaves, to garnish

MAKES 24

Blanch or steam the squash for 5 minutes, or until just tender.

Cut a thin slice off the base of each squash to allow it to stand upright, then slice a thin piece off the top to make a lid. Using a melon baller, scoop out the flesh from the squash, leaving a thin shell. Discard the flesh.

Heat the oil in a wok, then add the curry paste, spring onion and red capsicum and stir-fry for 2–3 minutes. Add the rice and stir-fry for a further 2–3 minutes. Add the chopped coriander and makrut leaves and toss to combine.

Remove from the heat and spoon 1 teaspoon of rice into each of the yellow squash. Garnish each with a coriander leaf and gently arrange the lids on top. Arrange on a platter and serve.

PREPARATION TIME: 20 MINUTES   COOKING TIME: 15 MINUTES

NOTES: For 185 g (6½ oz/1 cup) jasmine rice, you will need to cook 65 g (2¼ oz/⅓ cup) of rice in boiling water for about 10 minutes.
    The filling and squash can be prepared a day ahead. Cover and store separately in the refrigerator.

STUFFED CHERRY TOMATOES

16 cherry tomatoes
50 g (1¾ oz) goat's cheese
50 g (1¾ oz) ricotta cheese
2 prosciutto slices, finely chopped

MAKES 16

Slice the tops from the tomatoes, hollow out and discard the seeds. Turn them upside-down on paper towel and drain for a few minutes.

Beat together the goat's cheese and ricotta until smooth. Mix in the prosciutto, then season. Spoon into the tomatoes and refrigerate until needed.

PREPARATION TIME: 15 MINUTES +   COOKING TIME: NIL

Baby squash with rice stuffing

FORK FOOD

MARINATED RED CAPSICUM

3 red capsicums (peppers)
3 thyme sprigs
1 garlic clove, thinly sliced
2 teaspoons roughly chopped flat-leaf
(Italian) parsley
1 bay leaf
1 spring onion (scallion), sliced
1 teaspoon paprika
60 ml (2 fl oz/$\frac{1}{4}$ cup) extra virgin olive oil
2 tablespoons red wine vinegar

SERVES 6

Preheat the grill (broiler). Cut the capsicums into quarters and grill, skin side up, until the skin is black and blistered. Cool in a plastic bag, then peel. Slice thinly, then put in a bowl with the thyme, garlic, parsley, bay leaf and spring onion. Mix well.

Whisk together the paprika, oil, vinegar and some salt and pepper. Pour over the capsicum mixture and toss to combine. Cover and refrigerate for at least 3 hours, or preferably overnight. Remove from the refrigerator about 30 minutes before serving.

PREPARATION TIME: 20 MINUTES +   COOKING TIME: 5 MINUTES

NOTE: The capsicum can be refrigerated for up to 3 days.

MARINATED FETA CHEESE

350 g (12 oz) feta cheese
1 tablespoon dried oregano
1 teaspoon coriander seeds
125 g (4$\frac{1}{2}$ oz) sun-dried tomatoes in oil
4 small red chillies
3–4 rosemary sprigs
olive oil

SERVES 6–8

Pat the feta cheese dry with paper towels and cut into 2 cm ($\frac{3}{4}$ inch) cubes. Transfer to a bowl and sprinkle the oregano, coriander seeds and 1 tablespoon cracked black pepper all over the feta cheese.

Drain the sun-dried tomatoes over a bowl so that you retain all of the oil. Arrange the feta, chillies, rosemary and sun-dried tomatoes in a sterilized 750 ml (26 fl oz/3-cup) wide-necked jar with a clip-top lid. Cover with the reserved sun-dried tomato oil (you should have about 60 ml/2 fl oz/ $\frac{1}{4}$ cup) and top up with olive oil. Seal and refrigerate for 1 week before using. Serve at room temperature.

PREPARATION TIME: 10 MINUTES +   COOKING TIME: NIL

NOTES: To sterilize a storage jar, rinse with boiling water, then put in a very slow oven until completely dry.

The oil in the bottle will partly solidify when refrigerated, but will liquify when returned to room temperature.

The marinated feta will keep in the refrigerator for 1–2 months. Use the oil to make salad dressings or to flavour pasta.

ARTICHOKES IN AROMATIC VINAIGRETTE

2 tablespoons lemon juice
4 large globe artichokes
2 garlic cloves, crushed
1 teaspoon finely chopped oregano
1/2 teaspoon ground cumin
1/2 teaspoon ground coriander
pinch dried chilli flakes
3 teaspoons sherry vinegar
60 ml (2 fl oz/1/4 cup) olive oil

SERVES 4

Add the lemon juice to a large bowl of cold water. Trim the artichokes, cutting off the stalks to within 5 cm (2 inches) of the base of each artichoke and removing the tough outer leaves. Cut off the top quarter of the leaves from each. Slice each artichoke in half from top to base, or into quarters if large. Remove each small, furry choke with a teaspoon, then put each artichoke in the bowl of acidulated water to prevent it from discolouring while you prepare the rest.

Bring a large non-reactive saucepan of water to the boil, add the artichokes and a teaspoon of salt and simmer for 20 minutes, or until tender. The cooking time will depend on the artichoke size. Test by pressing a skewer into the base. If cooked, the artichoke should be soft and give little resistance. Strain, then put the artichokes on their cut side to drain while cooling.

To make the vinaigrette, combine the garlic, oregano, cumin, coriander and chilli flakes in a small bowl. Season and blend in the vinegar. Beating constantly, slowly pour in the olive oil to form an emulsion.

Arrange the artichokes in rows on a serving platter. Pour the vinaigrette over the top and allow to cool completely.

PREPARATION TIME: 20 MINUTES +   COOKING TIME: 20 MINUTES

MARINATED YOGHURT CHEESE BALLS

500 g (1 lb 2 oz/2 cups) Greek-style yoghurt
2 teaspoons sea salt
1 tablespoon dried oregano
2 teaspoons dried thyme
350 ml (12 fl oz/1⅓ cups) olive oil
1 bay leaf

MAKES 12

Fold a 30 x 60 cm (12 x 24 inch) piece of muslin (cheesecloth) in half to make a 30 cm (12 inch) square.

Combine the yoghurt, salt and 1 teaspoon black pepper in a bowl. Line a bowl with the muslin and spoon the mixture into the centre. Bring the corners together and, using a piece of kitchen string, tie as closely as possible to the yoghurt, leaving a loop at the end. Thread the loop through the handle of a wooden spoon and hang over a bowl to drain in the fridge for 3 days.

Combine the oregano and thyme in a shallow bowl. Pour half the oil into a 500 ml (17 fl oz/2-cup) jar and add the bay leaf.

Roll level tablespoons of the yoghurt into balls. Toss in the combined herbs and put into the jar of oil. Pour in the remaining oil to cover the balls completely. Seal and refrigerate for at least 1 day. Serve at room temperature, with chunky bread.

PREPARATION TIME: 20 MINUTES +   COOKING TIME: NIL

MARINATED MUSHROOMS

250 ml (9 fl oz/1 cup) apple cider vinegar
125 ml (4 fl oz/½ cup) orange juice
1 tablespoon coriander seeds
4 rosemary sprigs
2 bay leaves
500 g (1 lb 2 oz) button mushrooms
80 ml (2½ fl oz/⅓ cup) olive oil

SERVES 4

Put the apple cider vinegar, orange juice, coriander seeds, two rosemary sprigs and one bay leaf in a saucepan and bring to boil. Add the button mushrooms and simmer for 3 minutes. Remove and spoon into a sterilized jar. Boil the liquid until reduced by half. Discard the rosemary sprigs and bay leaf and replace with fresh ones.

Stir in the olive oil. Pour the liquid over the mushrooms and seal with a layer of olive oil. Will keep, refrigerated, for 1 month.

PREPARATION TIME: 10 MINUTES   COOKING TIME: 15 MINUTES

Marinated yoghurt cheese balls

TABOULEH

130 g (4^1/$_2$ oz/ ^{3}/$_4$ cup) burghul (bulgur)
3 ripe tomatoes
1 telegraph (long) cucumber
4 spring onions (scallions), sliced
120 g (4 oz) flat-leaf (Italian) parsley, chopped
2 large handfuls mint, chopped

DRESSING
80 ml (2^1/$_2$ fl oz/^{1}/$_3$ cup) lemon juice
60 ml (2 fl oz/^{1}/$_4$ cup) olive oil
1 tablespoon extra virgin olive oil

SERVES 6

Put the burghul in a bowl, cover with 500 ml (17 fl oz/2 cups) water and leave for 1^1/$_2$ hours.

Cut the tomatoes in half, squeeze to remove any excess seeds and cut into 1 cm (^{1}/$_2$ inch) cubes. Cut the cucumber in half lengthways, remove the seeds with a teaspoon and cut the flesh into 1 cm (^{1}/$_2$ inch) cubes.

To make the dressing, put the lemon juice and 1^1/$_2$ teaspoons salt in a bowl and whisk until well combined. Season well with freshly ground black pepper and slowly whisk in the olive oil and extra virgin olive oil.

Drain the burghul and squeeze out any excess water. Spread the burghul out on a tea towel (dish towel) or paper towels and leave to dry for about 30 minutes. Put the burghul in a large salad bowl, add the tomato, cucumber, spring onion, parsley and mint, and toss well to combine. Pour the dressing over the salad and toss until evenly coated.

PREPARATION TIME: 20 MINUTES +   COOKING TIME: NIL

ANTIPASTO SALAD

200 g (7 oz) sun-dried tomatoes
200 g (7 oz) marinated black olives
200 g (7 oz) marinated eggplant
(aubergine), chopped
200 g (7 oz) marinated artichokes
200 g (7 oz) sun-dried capsicum (pepper)
3 tablespoons chopped basil
balsamic vinegar, for drizzling

SERVES 4–6

Combine the sun-dried tomatoes, olives, eggplant, artichoke and capsicum. Toss through the basil. Drizzle with a little balsamic vinegar.

PREPARATION TIME: 10 MINUTES COOKING TIME: NIL

SESAME COLESLAW

¼ red cabbage
¼ green cabbage
100 g (3½ oz) snow peas (mangetout)
2 celery stalks
2 carrots
1 red capsicum (pepper)
whole-egg mayonnaise, to serve
1 small handful mint, finely
shredded, to serve
toasted sesame seeds, to serve

SERVES 4

Finely shred the red cabbage and green cabbage. Cut the snow peas, celery stalks, carrots and capsicum into strips.

Combine the cabbage and other vegetables in a large bowl and toss through enough whole-egg mayonnaise to lightly dress the salad. Top with finely shredded mint leaves and toasted sesame seeds.

PREPARATION TIME: 15 MINUTES COOKING TIME: NIL

Antipasto salad

HERBED POTATO SALAD

650 g (1 lb 7 oz) red-skinned potatoes
1 red onion, thinly sliced
1 tablespoon chopped mint
1 tablespoon chopped flat-leaf (Italian)
parsley
1 tablespoon snipped chives
90 g (3^{1}/$_4$ oz/^{1}/$_3$ cup) whole-egg
mayonnaise
90 g (3^{1}/$_4$ oz/^{1}/$_3$ cup) plain yoghurt

SERVES 4

Scrub the potatoes and cut into cubes. Cook in a large saucepan of boiling water until just tender, then drain and allow to cool completely.

Put the potatoes, onion and herbs in a large bowl. Combine the mayonnaise and yoghurt, then gently mix through to coat the potato, taking care not to break it up too much. Serve at room temperature.

PREPARATION TIME: 15 MINUTES   COOKING TIME: 15 MINUTES

AVOCADO AND BLACK BEAN SALAD

250 g (9 oz) dried black beans
1 red onion, chopped
4 roma (plum) tomatoes, chopped
1 red capsicum (pepper), chopped
375 g (13 oz) tinned corn kernels, drained
90 g (3¼ oz) coriander (cilantro) leaves, chopped
2 avocados, chopped
1 mango, peeled and chopped
150 g (5½ oz) rocket (arugula)

DRESSING
1 garlic clove, crushed
1 small red chilli, finely chopped
2 tablespoons lime juice
60 ml (2 fl oz/¼ cup) olive oil

SERVES 4

Soak the beans in cold water overnight. Rinse, then drain. Put the beans into a large heavy-based saucepan, cover with water and bring to the boil. Reduce the heat and simmer for 1½ hours, or until tender. Drain and cool slightly.

Put the beans, onion, tomatoes, capsicum, corn, coriander, avocado, mango and rocket into a large bowl and toss to combine.

To make the dressing, combine all the ingredients in a bowl and whisk. Pour over the salad and toss.

PREPARATION TIME: 15 MINUTES +   COOKING TIME: 1 HOUR 30 MINUTES

SPICY POTATO SALAD

500 g (1 lb 2 oz) baby new potatoes, halved
250 g (9 oz) green beans, trimmed, tailed and halved diagonally

DRESSING
60 ml (2 fl oz/¼ cup) olive oil
2 red chillies, seeded and sliced
1 garlic clove, crushed
1 large handful coriander (cilantro) leaves, chopped
1 tablespoon red wine vinegar
½ teaspoon caraway seeds

SERVES 6

Cook the potatoes in a large saucepan of gently simmering water for 20 minutes, or until tender but still firm. Drain and set aside.

Blanch the beans in boiling water for 2 minutes, or until bright green and just tender. Drain the beans and set aside.

To make the dressing, whisk all the ingredients in a small bowl until well combined. Pour the dressing over the combined beans and potatoes and serve immediately.

PREPARATION TIME: 15 MINUTES   COOKING TIME: 15 MINUTES

Avocado and black bean salad

CANNELLINI BEAN SALAD

425 g (15 oz) tinned cannellini beans
1 tomato, finely chopped
3 anchovy fillets, sliced
1 tablespoon finely chopped red onion
2 teaspoons finely chopped basil
2 teaspoons extra virgin olive oil
1 teaspoon balsamic vinegar
crusty bread, cut into slices, to serve
olive oil, for brushing
1 garlic clove, bruised

SERVES 6–8

Rinse and drain the cannellini beans.

Combine the cannellini beans, tomato, anchovies, onion, basil, olive oil and balsamic vinegar.

Lightly brush the slices of bread with the oil, then toast and rub with the garlic. Spoon the salad onto the bread slices to serve.

PREPARATION TIME: 20 MINUTES   COOKING TIME: 5 MINUTES

NOTE: The salad can be prepared up to a day ahead, covered and refrigerated.

FAST MELON SALAD

1 large honeydew melon
60 g (2¼ oz/2 cups) watercress sprigs, trimmed
2 avocados, sliced
1 large red capsicum (pepper), thinly sliced
220 g (7¾ oz) marinated feta cheese, crumbled into large chunks
90 g (3¼ oz) marinated niçoise olives

DRESSING
60 ml (2 fl oz/¼ cup) olive oil
2 tablespoons white wine vinegar
1 teaspoon dijon mustard

SERVES 4–6

Cut the honeydew melon into slices and arrange on a large platter. Scatter the watercress sprigs over the top. Arrange on top the avocado, capsicum, feta cheese and niçoise olives.

To make the dressing, put the olive oil, white wine vinegar and dijon mustard in a screw-top jar and shake until well combined. Drizzle over the salad.

PREPARATION TIME: 15 MINUTES   COOKING TIME: NIL

PEACH SALSA SALAD

6 large peaches, cut into wedges
1 red onion, thinly sliced
6 roma (plum) tomatoes, quartered
200 g (7 oz/1 cup) corn kernels
1 green capsicum (pepper), sliced
1 large handful coriander (cilantro) leaves

DRESSING
1 garlic clove, crushed
1 teaspoon ground cumin
1 red chilli, finely chopped
2 tablespoons freshly squeezed lime juice
60 ml (2 fl oz/¼ cup) oil

SERVES 4–6

Put the peaches, onion, tomatoes, corn kernels and capsicum in a bowl.

To make the dressing, mix together the garlic, cumin, chilli, lime juice and oil. Pour over the salad and toss to combine. Fold through the coriander leaves just before serving.

PREPARATION TIME: 15 MINUTES   COOKING TIME: NIL

Fast melon salad

RUSSIAN SALAD

MAYONNAISE
2 egg yolks
1 teaspoon dijon mustard
125 ml (4 fl oz/^{1}/$_2$ cup) extra virgin
olive oil
2 tablespoons lemon juice
2 small garlic cloves, crushed

3 tinned globe artichoke hearts
3 waxy potatoes, such as desiree,
unpeeled
100 g (3^1/$_2$ oz) baby green beans, trimmed
and cut into 1 cm (^{1}/$_2$ inch) lengths
1 large carrot, cut into 1 cm (^{1}/$_2$ inch)
cubes
125 g (4^1/$_2$ oz) fresh peas
30 g (1 oz) cornichons, chopped
2 tablespoons baby capers, rinsed and
drained
10 black olives, cut into 3 slices
4 anchovy fillets, finely chopped
black olives, to garnish

SERVES 4–6

To make the mayonnaise, beat the egg yolks with the mustard and
^{1}/$_4$ teaspoon salt using electric beaters until creamy. Gradually add the
oil in a fine stream, beating constantly until all the oil has been added.
Add the lemon juice, garlic and 1 teaspoon boiling water and beat for
1 minute until well combined. Season, to taste.

Cut each artichoke into quarters. Rinse the potatoes, cover with cold
salted water and bring to a gentle simmer. Cook for 15–20 minutes, or
until tender when pierced with a knife. Drain and allow to cool slightly.
Peel and set aside. When the potatoes are completely cool, cut into
1 cm (^{1}/$_2$ inch) cubes.

Blanch the beans in boiling salted water until tender but still firm to
the bite. Refresh in cold water, then drain thoroughly. Repeat with the
carrot and peas.

Set aside a small quantity of each vegetable, including the cornichons,
for the garnish and season, to taste. Put the remainder in a bowl with the
capers, anchovies and sliced olives. Add the mayonnaise, toss to
combine and season to taste. Arrange on a serving dish and garnish with
the reserved vegetables and the whole olives.

PREPARATION TIME: 40 MINUTES +   COOKING TIME: 40 MINUTES

NOTE: This salad can be prepared up to 2 days in advance and
stored in the refrigerator but should be served at room temperature.

PRAWN AND PAPAYA SALAD WITH LIME DRESSING

750 g (1 lb 10 oz) cooked prawns (shrimp)
1 large papaya, chopped
1 small red onion, thinly sliced
2 celery stalks, thinly sliced
2 tablespoons shredded mint

LIME DRESSING
125 ml (4 fl oz/½ cup) oil
60 ml (2 fl oz/¼ cup) lime juice
2 teaspoons finely grated fresh ginger
1 teaspoon caster (superfine) sugar

SERVES 4

Peel the prawns, leaving the tails intact. Gently pull out the dark vein from each prawn back, starting from the head end. Put the prawns in a bowl.

To make the lime dressing, put the oil, lime juice, ginger and sugar in a small bowl and whisk to combine. Season.

Add the lime dressing to the prawns and gently toss to coat the prawns. Add the papaya, onion, celery and mint and gently toss to combine. Serve the salad at room temperature, or cover and refrigerate for up to 3 hours before serving.

PREPARATION TIME: 25 MINUTES   COOKING TIME: NIL

MARINATED MUSHROOM SALAD

500 g (1 lb 2 oz) button mushrooms, halved
4 spring onions (scallions), thinly sliced
1 red capsicum (pepper), finely diced
2 tablespoons chopped flat-leaf (Italian) parsley

DRESSING
3 garlic cloves, crushed
60 ml (2 fl oz/¼ cup) white wine vinegar
2 teaspoons dijon mustard
80 ml (2½ fl oz/⅓ cup) olive oil

SERVES 4–6

Combine the mushrooms, spring onion, capsicum and parsley in a large bowl.

To make the dressing, combine the garlic, white wine vinegar, dijon mustard and olive oil. Pour the dressing over the mushrooms and toss to coat. Cover and refrigerate for 3 hours before serving.

PREPARATION TIME: 10 MINUTES +   COOKING TIME: NIL

Prawn and papaya salad with lime dressing

CHICKEN AND VEGETABLE SALAD

400 g (14 oz) boneless, skinless chicken breast

3 slices fresh ginger

2 lemon grass stems (white part only), roughly chopped

2 tablespoons fish sauce

250 g (9 oz) broccoli, cut into florets

150 g (5$\frac{1}{2}$ oz) baby corn

100 g (3$\frac{1}{2}$ oz) snow peas (mangetout), trimmed

1 red capsicum (pepper), cut into strips

3 spring onions (scallions), cut into strips

125 ml (4 fl oz/$\frac{1}{2}$ cup) sweet chilli sauce

2 tablespoons honey

2 tablespoons lime juice

2 teaspoons grated lime zest

1 handful coriander (cilantro) leaves

SERVES 4–6

Slice the chicken into short, thin strips.

Put the ginger, lemon grass, fish sauce and 250 ml (9 fl oz/1 cup) water in a frying pan. Bring the mixture to the boil, reduce the heat slightly and simmer for 5 minutes.

Add the chicken to the pan and cook in the hot liquid for 5 minutes, stirring occasionally. Drain and allow to cool. Discard the liquid.

Bring a large saucepan of water to the boil and cook the broccoli, corn, snow peas, capsicum and spring onion for 2 minutes. Drain and plunge into iced water, then drain again.

Combine the sweet chilli sauce, honey, lime juice and zest in a small bowl and mix well. Arrange the vegetables and chicken on a serving platter. Pour the sauce over the top and gently toss. Sprinkle with the coriander leaves.

PREPARATION TIME: 30 MINUTES   COOKING TIME: 20 MINUTES

NOTE: To trim snow peas, cut or break both ends off and then pull away any strings from along the sides.

SALATA BALADI

2 tablespoons extra virgin olive oil
2 tablespoons lemon juice
1 cos (romaine) lettuce, torn into
bite-sized pieces
3 ripe tomatoes, each cut into 8 pieces
1 green capsicum (pepper), cut into
bite-sized pieces
1 telegraph (long) cucumber, seeded and
chopped
6 radishes, sliced
1 small red onion, thinly sliced
2 tablespoons chopped flat-leaf (Italian)
parsley
2 tablespoons chopped mint

SERVES 4–6

In a bowl, whisk together the olive oil and lemon juice. Season well.

Combine the remaining ingredients in a large serving bowl and toss well. Add the dressing and toss to combine.

PREPARATION TIME: 10 MINUTES   COOKING TIME: NIL

NOTE: Salad onions are sweeter than normal onions and are readily available.

CUCUMBER SALAD WITH PEANUTS AND CHILLI

3 Lebanese (short) cucumbers
2 tablespoons white vinegar
2 teaspoons sugar
1–2 tablespoons chilli sauce
1/2 red onion, chopped
1 large handful coriander (cilantro)
leaves
160 g (5³/4 oz/1 cup) unsalted roasted
peanuts, chopped
2 tablespoons crisp fried garlic
1/2 teaspoon chopped chilli
1 tablespoon fish sauce

SERVES 4–6

Peel the cucumbers and slice in half lengthways. Remove the seeds with a teaspoon and slice thinly.

Combine the vinegar and sugar in a small bowl, and stir until the sugar dissolves. Transfer to a large bowl and toss with the cucumber, chilli sauce, onion and coriander. Allow to marinate for 45 minutes.

Just before serving, add the peanuts, garlic, chilli and fish sauce. Toss lightly to combine.

PREPARATION TIME: 25 MINUTES +   COOKING TIME: NIL

COLD VEGETABLE SALAD WITH SPICE DRESSING

300 g (10½ oz) green or snake (yard-long) beans
10 English spinach leaves
80 g (2¾ oz) snow pea (mangetout) sprouts
1 red capsicum (pepper)
1 red onion
100 g (3½ oz) bean sprouts, trimmed

SPICE DRESSING
2 tablespoons peanut oil
1 garlic clove, crushed
1 teaspoon grated fresh ginger
1 small red chilli, chopped
2 tablespoons desiccated coconut
1 tablespoon brown vinegar

SERVES 4

Top and tail the beans and cut them into 10 cm (4 inch) lengths. Remove the stems from the spinach leaves and slice the leaves thinly. Remove about 1 cm (½ inch) of the long stems from the snow pea sprouts. Cut the capsicum into thin strips. Thinly slice the onion.

Put the beans in a large saucepan of boiling water and cook for 1 minute to blanch, then drain. Combine the beans, spinach, snow pea sprouts, bean sprouts, capsicum and onion in a bowl.

To make the spice dressing, heat the oil in a small frying pan. Add the garlic, ginger, chilli and coconut, and stir-fry over medium heat for 1 minute. Add the vinegar and 80 ml (2½ fl oz/⅓ cup) water, and simmer for 1 minute. Allow to cool.

To serve, add the dressing to the vegetables, and toss until combined.

PREPARATION TIME: 15 MINUTES +   COOKING TIME: 10 MINUTES

NOTES: Snow pea sprouts are the growing tips and tendrils from the snow pea plant.

Any blanched vegetables can be used in this salad. Try to use a variety of vegetables which result in a colourful appearance.

The spice dressing can be added up to 30 minutes before serving.

TUNA, GREEN BEAN AND ONION SALAD

200 g (7 oz) green beans, trimmed and cut into short lengths
300 g (10½ oz) penne rigate
125 ml (4 fl oz/½ cup) olive oil
250 g (9 oz) tuna steak, cut into thick slices
1 red onion, thinly sliced
1 tablespoon balsamic vinegar

SERVES 4

In a large saucepan of boiling water, cook the prepared beans for 1–2 minutes, or until tender but still crisp. Remove with a slotted spoon and rinse under cold water. Drain and transfer to a serving bowl.

Cook the pasta in a saucepan of boiling salted water until *al dente*. Drain, rinse under cold water and drain again before adding to the beans.

Heat half the oil in a frying pan. Add the tuna and onion and gently sauté until the tuna is just cooked through. Stir the tuna carefully to prevent it from breaking up. Add the vinegar, increase the heat to high and briefly cook until the dressing has reduced and lightly coats the tuna. Transfer the tuna and onion to a bowl.

Toss the beans, pasta, tuna and onion together and mix with the remaining oil, and season to taste. Allow to cool before serving.

PREPARATION TIME: 20 MINUTES   COOKING TIME: 15 MINUTES

TUNA AND WHITE BEAN SALAD

750 g (1 lb 10 oz) tinned tuna in oil
400 g (14 oz) tinned cannellini beans, drained and rinsed
1 large red onion, coarsely chopped
3 hard-boiled eggs, cut into wedges
3 tomatoes, cut into wedges

DRESSING
1 garlic clove, crushed
1–2 teaspoons thyme
1–2 teaspoons finely chopped flat-leaf (Italian) parsley
60 ml (2 fl oz/¼ cup) white wine vinegar
80 ml (2½ fl oz/⅓ cup) extra virgin olive oil

SERVES 4–6

Drain the tuna and flake into chunks.

To make the dressing, combine the garlic, thyme, parsley, vinegar and olive oil in a bowl and whisk. Season.

Combine the beans and onion in a large bowl. Add the dressing and toss. Add the tuna, toss gently, then add half the egg wedges and half the tomato. Lightly combine. Pile on a platter and garnish with the remaining egg and tomato.

PREPARATION TIME: 15 MINUTES   COOKING TIME: NIL

Tuna, green bean and onion salad

FISH AND HERB SALAD

500 g (1 lb 2 oz) smoked cod
60 ml (2 fl oz/¼ cup) lime juice
30 g (1 oz/½ cup) flaked coconut
200 g (7 oz/1 cup) jasmine rice, cooked
and cooled
25 g (1 oz) Vietnamese mint, chopped
3 tablespoons chopped mint
25 g (1 oz) chopped coriander (cilantro)
leaves
8 makrut (kaffir lime) leaves, very finely
shredded

DRESSING
1 tablespoon chopped coriander
(cilantro) root
2 cm (¾ inch) piece fresh ginger,
finely grated
1 red chilli, finely chopped
1 tablespoon chopped lemon grass,
white part only
3 tablespoons chopped Thai basil
1 avocado, chopped
80 ml (2½ fl oz/⅓ cup) lime juice
2 tablespoons fish sauce
1 teaspoon soft brown sugar
125 ml (4 fl oz/½ cup) peanut oil

SERVES 4–6

Preheat the oven to 150°C (300°F/Gas 2). Put the cod in a large frying pan and cover with water. Add the lime juice and simmer for 15 minutes, or until the fish flakes when tested with a fork. Drain and set aside to cool slightly before breaking it into bite-sized pieces.

Meanwhile, spread the coconut onto a baking tray and toast in the oven for 10 minutes, or until golden brown, shaking the tray occasionally. Remove the coconut from the tray to prevent it burning.

Put the fish, coconut, rice, Vietnamese mint, mint, coriander and makrut leaves in a large bowl and mix to combine.

To make the dressing, put the coriander root, ginger, chilli, lemon grass and basil in a food processor and process until combined. Add the avocado, lime juice, fish sauce, sugar and peanut oil and process until creamy. Pour the dressing over the salad and toss to coat the rice and fish. Serve immediately.

PREPARATION TIME: 40 MINUTES   COOKING TIME: 15 MINUTES

LARB

1 tablespoon oil

2 lemon grass stems, white part only, thinly sliced

2 green chillies, finely chopped

500 g (1 lb 2 oz) lean minced (ground) pork or beef

60 ml (2 fl oz/^{1}/4 cup) lime juice

2 teaspoons finely grated lime zest

2–6 teaspoons chilli sauce

lettuce leaves, to serve

3 tablespoons chopped coriander (cilantro) leaves

2 tablespoons chopped mint

1 small red onion, thinly sliced

50 g (1^3/4 oz/^{1}/3 cup) unsalted roasted peanuts, chopped

25 g (1 oz/^{1}/4 cup) crisp fried garlic

SERVES 4–6

Heat the oil in a wok and stir-fry the lemon grass, chilli and pork or beef over high heat for 6 minutes, or until the meat is cooked, breaking up any lumps. Transfer to a bowl and allow to cool.

Add the lime juice, zest and chilli sauce to the pork or beef mixture. Arrange the lettuce leaves on a serving plate. Stir most of the coriander, mint, onion, peanuts and fried garlic through the mixture, spoon over the lettuce and sprinkle the rest of the coriander, mint, onion, peanuts and garlic over the top.

PREPARATION TIME: 20 MINUTES +   COOKING TIME: 10 MINUTES

MIXED VEGETABLE SALAD

300 g (10^1/2 oz) pineapple, chopped

1 telegraph (long) cucumber, chopped

250 g (9 oz) cherry tomatoes, halved

155 g (5^1/2 oz) green beans, thinly sliced

155 g (5^1/2 oz) bean sprouts, trimmed

80 ml (2^1/2 fl oz/^{1}/3 cup) rice vinegar

2 tablespoons lime juice

2 red chillies, seeded and very finely chopped

2 teaspoons sugar

30 g (1 oz) dried shrimp, to garnish

small mint leaves, to garnish

SERVES 4–6

Toss together the pineapple, cucumber, tomatoes, beans and sprouts in a bowl. Cover and refrigerate until chilled. Combine the vinegar, lime juice, chilli and sugar in a small bowl and stir until the sugar dissolves.

Dry-fry the shrimp in a frying pan, shaking the pan constantly until the shrimp are light orange and fragrant. Process the shrimp in a food processor until finely chopped.

Arrange the chilled salad on a serving platter, drizzle the dressing over the top and garnish with the chopped shrimp and mint leaves. Serve immediately.

PREPARATION TIME: 40 MINUTES   COOKING TIME: 5 MINUTES

WATERCRESS AND DUCK SALAD WITH LYCHEES

2 large duck breasts, skin on
1 tablespoon soy sauce
1/2 each red, green and yellow capsicum
(pepper)
250 g (9 oz) watercress
12 fresh or canned lychees
2 tablespoons pickled shredded ginger
1–2 tablespoons green peppercorns
(optional)
1 tablespoon white vinegar
2 teaspoons soft brown sugar
1–2 teaspoons chopped red chilli
1 large handful coriander (cilantro)
leaves

Preheat the oven to 210°C (415°F/Gas 6–7). Brush the duck breasts with the soy sauce and put on a rack in a baking tin. Bake for 30 minutes. Remove from the oven and allow to cool.

Slice the capsicums into thin strips. Discard any tough woody stems from the watercress. Peel the fresh lychees and remove the seeds. If you are using canned lychees, drain them thoroughly.

Arrange the capsicum strips, watercress, lychees and ginger on a large serving platter. Slice the duck into thin pieces and toss gently through the salad.

In a small bowl, combine the peppercorns, if using, vinegar, sugar, chilli and coriander. Serve this on the side for spooning over the salad.

SERVES 4   PREPARATION TIME: 25 MINUTES +   COOKING TIME: 30 MINUTES

EGGPLANT SALAD

1 kg (2 lb 4 oz) large eggplants (aubergines)
125 ml (4 fl oz/1/2 cup) olive oil
1 onion, finely chopped
1/2 teaspoon ground cinnamon
4 garlic cloves, crushed
800 g (1 lb 12 oz) tinned crushed tomatoes
2 tablespoons chopped coriander (cilantro) leaves
3 tablespoons chopped flat-leaf (Italian) parsley
1 tablespoon lemon juice
2 tablespoons chopped mint
150 g (5½ oz) Greek-style yoghurt
25 g (1 oz) pine nuts, toasted

SERVES 6

Cut the eggplants into 2 cm (3/4 inch) cubes. Put in a colander and leave to stand over a bowl and sprinkle generously with salt. Leave for 30 minutes, rinse under cold water, then pat dry with a tea towel (dish towel).

Heat 2 tablespoons of the oil in a large frying pan and fry batches of eggplant until golden, adding more oil if necessary. Drain on paper towels.

Heat another 2 tablespoons of the oil in the pan and fry the onion for 1 minute. Add the cinnamon and half the garlic, cook for 1 minute, then add the tomato. Add the eggplant and simmer, uncovered, for 1 hour, or until the mixture is quite dry. Add half of each of the coriander and parsley. Stir and leave to cool.

Mix 2 tablespoons of oil with the lemon juice and add the remaining crushed garlic and the mint. Stir into the yoghurt.

Toss the pine nuts through the salad and garnish with the remaining fresh herbs. Serve at room temperature with the garlic yoghurt dressing.

PREPARATION TIME: 20 MINUTES +   COOKING TIME: 1 HOUR 35 MINUTES

BACON, LETTUCE AND TOMATO SALAD

4 bacon slices
1 cos (romaine) lettuce
200 g (7 oz) cherry tomatoes, halved
1 avocado, chopped

DRESSING
125 g (4½ oz/1/2 cup) plain yoghurt
1 tablespoon wholegrain mustard
1 tablespoon lemon juice
1 teaspoon honey

SERVES 4

Fry the bacon in a frying pan over medium heat until crisp. Allow to cool on paper towels before roughly chopping.

Put the bacon in a bowl together with the lettuce, tomatoes and avocado. Toss gently to combine.

To make the dressing, mix together the yoghurt, mustard, lemon juice and honey. Drizzle over the salad and toss to combine.

PREPARATION TIME: 10 MINUTES   COOKING TIME: 10 MINUTES

Eggplant salad

GADO GADO

6 new potatoes
2 carrots, cut into batons
250 g (9 oz) snake (yard-long) beans,
trimmed and cut into 10 cm
(4 inch) lengths
2 tablespoons peanut oil
250 g (9 oz) firm tofu, cubed
100 g (3^1/$_2$ oz) baby English spinach
leaves
2 Lebanese (short) cucumbers, cut into
thick strips
1 large red capsicum (pepper), cut into
thick strips
100 g (3^1/$_2$ oz) bean sprouts, trimmed
5 hard-boiled eggs, cut in half

PEANUT SAUCE
1 tablespoon peanut oil
1 onion, finely chopped
160 g (5^3/$_4$ oz/^{2}/$_3$ cup) peanut butter
60 ml (2 fl oz/^{1}/$_4$ cup) kecap manis
2 tablespoons ground coriander
2 teaspoons chilli sauce
185 ml (6 fl oz/^{3}/$_4$ cup) coconut cream
1 teaspoon grated palm sugar (jaggery) or
soft brown sugar
1 tablespoon lemon juice

SERVES 6–8

Cook the potatoes in a saucepan of boiling water until tender. Drain, cool slightly, then cut into quarters.

Cook the carrots and beans separately until just tender. Drain, plunge into iced water, then drain thoroughly.

Heat the oil in a non-stick frying pan and cook the tofu all over in batches until crisp. Drain on crumpled paper towels.

To make the peanut sauce, heat the oil in a frying pan over low heat and cook the onion for 5 minutes, or until golden. Add the peanut butter, kecap manis, coriander, chilli sauce and coconut cream. Bring to the boil, reduce the heat and simmer for 5 minutes. Stir in the sugar and lemon juice, stirring until dissolved.

Arrange all the vegetables, tofu and eggs on a plate around the bowl of sauce.

PREPARATION TIME: 30 MINUTES   COOKING TIME: 35 MINUTES

115

GARDEN SALAD

1 green oak-leaf lettuce
150 g (5½ oz) rocket (arugula)
1 small radicchio lettuce
1 large green capsicum (pepper), cut into thin strips
grated zest of 1 lemon

DRESSING
2 tablespoons roughly chopped coriander (cilantro) leaves
60 ml (2 fl oz/¼ cup) lemon juice
2 teaspoons soft brown sugar
2 tablespoons olive oil
1 garlic clove, crushed (optional)

SERVES 4–6

Tear the salad greens into bite-size pieces. Combine the salad greens, capsicum and lemon zest in a large serving bowl.

To make the dressing, whisk all the ingredients in a small bowl until well combined. Pour the dressing over the salad and toss to combine.

PREPARATION TIME: 15 MINUTES   COOKING TIME: NIL

NOTES: Make the dressing and salad just before serving. Choose a selection of your favourite salad greens for this recipe.
This is delicious served in summer with a chilled frascati or a light red wine.

BEETROOT AND NECTARINE SALAD

1.3 kg (3 lb/2 bunches) trimmed baby beetroot (beets)
4 nectarines
2 tablespoons sunflower seeds, toasted
2 tablespoons chervil

DRESSING
1 tablespoon wholegrain mustard
2 tablespoons raspberry vinegar
2 tablespoons honey
90 g (3¼ oz/⅓ cup) plain yoghurt
60 ml (2 fl oz/¼ cup) oil

SERVES 4–6

Boil, steam or microwave the beetroot until tender. Drain and allow to cool before cutting into quarters. Cut the nectarines into thick wedges. Combine the beetroot, nectarines, sunflower seeds and chervil leaves.

To make the dressing, mix together the mustard, vinegar, honey, yoghurt and oil. Drizzle the dressing over the salad just before serving.

PREPARATION TIME: 15 MINUTES   COOKING TIME: 15 MINUTES

Garden salad

MOROCCAN LAMB AND ROASTED CAPSICUM WITH FUSILLI

500 g (1 lb 2 oz) lamb fillets
3 teaspoons ground cumin
1 tablespoon ground coriander
2 teaspoons ground allspice
1 teaspoon ground cinnamon
1/2 teaspoon ground cayenne pepper
4 garlic cloves, crushed
80 ml (2 1/2 fl oz/1/3 cup) olive oil
125 ml (4 fl oz/1/2 cup) lemon juice
2 red capsicums (peppers)
400 g (14 oz) fusilli
60 ml (2 fl oz/1/4 cup) olive oil, extra
2 teaspoons harissa
150 g (5 1/2 oz) rocket (arugula)

SERVES 4–6

Cut the fillets in half if they are very long. Mix the cumin, coriander, allspice, cinnamon, cayenne, garlic, olive oil and half the lemon juice in a bowl. Add the lamb, stir to coat and marinate, covered, in the refrigerator overnight.

Preheat the grill (broiler). Cut the capsicums into large pieces and grill, skin side up, until the skin is black and blistered. Cool in a plastic bag, then peel. Slice thinly.

Cook the fusilli in a large saucepan of rapidly boiling salted water until al dente. Drain and keep warm.

Drain the lamb, heat 1 tablespoon of the extra virgin olive oil in a large frying pan and cook the lamb over high heat until done to your liking. Remove from the pan and cover with foil.

Heat 1 teaspoon of the oil in the frying pan and cook the harissa over medium heat for a few seconds. Be careful as the mixture may spit. Remove and put in a small screw-top jar with the remaining oil and lemon juice and shake the jar until well combined. Season to taste.

Thinly slice the lamb fillets and toss with the warm pasta, capsicum and rocket. Toss the harissa dressing through the pasta. Serve warm.

PREPARATION TIME: 25 MINUTES +   COOKING TIME: 25 MINUTES

CUCUMBER, FETA, MINT AND DILL SALAD

120 g (4 oz) feta cheese
4 Lebanese (short) cucumbers
1 small red onion, thinly sliced
1½ tablespoons finely chopped dill
1 tablespoon dried mint
60 ml (2 fl oz/¼ cup) olive oil
1½ tablespoons lemon juice

SERVES 4

Crumble the feta into 1 cm (½ inch) pieces and put in a large bowl. Peel and seed the cucumbers and cut into 1 cm (½ inch) cubes. Add to the bowl along with the onion and dill.

Grind the mint using a mortar and pestle, or force through a sieve, until powdered. Combine with the oil and juice, then season. Pour over the salad and toss well.

PREPARATION TIME: 15 MINUTES   COOKING TIME: NIL

CHEF'S SALAD

DRESSING
125 ml (4 fl oz/½ cup) extra virgin olive oil
2 tablespoons white wine vinegar
1 teaspoon sugar

1 iceberg lettuce
2 tomatoes, cut into wedges
2 celery stalks, cut into thin batons
1 cooked boneless, skinless chicken breast, cut into thin strips
200 g (7 oz) ham, cut into thin strips
60 g (2¼ oz) Swiss cheese, cut into strips
3 hard-boiled eggs, cut into wedges
6 radishes, sliced

SERVES 4

Whisk the dressing ingredients together in a bowl until well combined. Season to taste.

Roughly shred the lettuce leaves and divide among serving plates. Top with layers of the tomato, celery, chicken, ham, cheese, egg and radish. Drizzle the dressing over the salad and serve immediately.

PREPARATION TIME: 25 MINUTES   COOKING TIME: NIL

Cucumber, feta, mint and dill salad

FARFALLE SALAD WITH SUN-DRIED TOMATOES AND SPINACH

500 g (1 lb 2 oz) farfalle or spiral pasta
3 spring onions (scallions)
50 g (1³/₄ oz) sun-dried tomatoes, cut into strips
1 kg (2 lb 4 oz) English spinach, stalks trimmed and leaves shredded
50 g (1³/₄ oz/¹/₃ cup) pine nuts, toasted
1 tablespoon chopped oregano
60 ml (2 fl oz/¹/₄ cup) olive oil
1 teaspoon sliced chilli
1 garlic clove, crushed

SERVES 6

Cook the pasta in a large saucepan of rapidly boiling salted water until *al dente*. Drain, rinse under cold water and drain again. Allow to cool and transfer to a large salad bowl.

Trim the spring onions and thinly slice diagonally. Add to the pasta with the tomato, spinach, pine nuts and oregano.

To make the dressing, combine the oil, chilli, garlic and salt and pepper in a small screw-top jar and shake well. Pour the dressing over the top of the salad and toss to combine.

PREPARATION TIME: 20 MINUTES   COOKING TIME: 15 MINUTES

PASTRAMI, MUSHROOM AND CUCUMBER SALAD

200 g (7 oz) lasagnette, broken into quarters
250 g (9 oz) sliced pastrami, cut in strips
1 celery stalk, sliced
2 small tomatoes, cut into wedges
1 Lebanese (short) cucumber, thinly sliced
80 g (2³/4 oz) button mushrooms, sliced
1 tablespoon chopped coriander (cilantro) leaves

DRESSING
60 ml (2 fl oz/¹/4 cup) olive oil
2 tablespoons red wine vinegar
¹/2 teaspoon dijon mustard
1 garlic clove, crushed
¹/4 teaspoon hot chilli oil

SERVES 4

Cook the lasagnette in a large saucepan of rapidly boiling salted water until *al dente*. Drain, rinse under cold water and drain again. Allow to cool and transfer to a large salad bowl.

Add the pastrami, celery, tomato wedges, cucumber and mushrooms to the pasta.

To prepare the dressing, combine all the ingredients in a screw-top jar and shake until well blended.

Toss the dressing through the salad and refrigerate, covered, for several hours. Adjust the seasoning and sprinkle with the coriander before serving.

PREPARATION TIME: 20 MINUTES +   COOKING TIME: 10 MINUTES

TUNA AND PASTA SALAD

500 g (1 lb 2 oz) conchiglie (shell pasta)
200 g (7 oz) beans, trimmed
2 red capsicums (peppers), thinly sliced
2 spring onions (scallions), chopped
425 g (15 oz) tinned tuna, in oil
2 tablespoons olive oil
60 ml (2 fl oz/¹/4 cup) white wine vinegar
1 tablespoon lemon juice
1 garlic clove, crushed
1 teaspoon sugar
1 Lebanese (short) cucumber, thinly sliced
6 hard-boiled eggs, quartered
4 tomatoes, cut into eighths
80 g (2³/4 oz/¹/2 cup) black olives
2 tablespoons chopped basil

SERVES 6

Cook the pasta in a large saucepan of rapidly boiling salted water until *al dente*. Drain, rinse under cold water and drain again.

Cut the beans into short lengths. Combine the pasta, beans, capsicum and spring onion in a large bowl and mix well. Drain the tuna, reserving the oil, and flake with a fork.

Combine the reserved tuna oil, oil, vinegar, lemon juice, garlic and sugar in a small screw-top jar. Shake vigorously for 2 minutes, or until well combined.

Spoon the pasta into the centre of a large serving platter. Arrange the cucumber, egg and tomato around the edge of the platter, and drizzle with half the dressing. Scatter the flaked tuna, olives and basil over the salad and drizzle with the remaining dressing just before serving.

PREPARATION TIME: 20 MINUTES   COOKING TIME: 15 MINUTES

Pastrami, mushroom and cucumber salad

SPICED LAMB RICE

3 lamb shanks (about 1 kg/2 lb 4 oz)
1 large onion, sliced
10 whole cloves
1 cinnamon stick
5 cardamom pods
60 ml (2 fl oz/¼ cup) melted ghee or oil
1 teaspoon crushed garlic
2 onions, extra, thinly sliced,
¼ teaspoon ground cinnamon
¼ teaspoon ground cloves
¼ teaspoon freshly grated nutmeg
600 g (1 lb 5 oz/3 cups) long-grain white rice
¼ teaspoon saffron threads
currants, to garnish
shelled pistachios, to garnish

SERVES 4

Put the lamb in a large saucepan with the onion, cloves, cinnamon stick, cardamom pods, 2 litres (70 fl oz/8 cups) water and 1½ teaspoons salt. Bring to the boil. Simmer for 1–1½ hours, or until the meat is tender, occasionally skimming any scum off the surface. Remove the shanks from the cooking liquid, then cool slightly. Strain the remaining liquid into a large measuring cup — you need 1.25 litres (44 fl oz/5 cups). If necessary, add some water.

Heat the ghee or oil in a small saucepan and cook the garlic and extra onion gently until well reduced and just golden. Add the ground spices and ¼ teaspoon freshly ground black pepper.

Remove the meat from the shanks and cut into cubes. Put in a bowl with the onion and spice mixture.

Wash and drain the rice. Put half of it in a large saucepan with a tight-fitting lid and cover with the onion and lamb mixture. Put the remaining rice on top.

Cook the saffron threads in a dry frying pan over a low heat until dry and crisp, stirring constantly. Allow to cool. Put the strands in a bowl and crush with the back of a spoon. Add 60 ml (2 fl oz/¼ cup) water and dissolve.

Gently pour the reserved cooking liquid and dissolved saffron into the saucepan with the rice and lamb mixture and bring to the boil. Cover, reduce the heat to very low and cook for 20 minutes. Remove the lid, then lightly fluff up the rice. Serve at room temperature, garnished with currants and pistachios.

PREPARATION TIME: 30 MINUTES   COOKING TIME: 2 HOURS

GREEN PAPAYA SALAD

370 g (13 oz) green papaya, peeled and seeded
90 g (3¼ oz) snake beans, trimmed and cut into 2 cm (¾ inch) lengths
2 garlic cloves
2 small red chillies, chopped
5 teaspoons dried shrimp
8 cherry tomatoes, halved
50 g (1¾ oz) coriander (cilantro) sprigs
40 g (1½ oz/¼ cup) chopped roasted peanuts

DRESSING
60 ml (2 fl oz/¼ cup) fish sauce
2 tablespoons tamarind purée
1 tablespoon lime juice
3 tablespoons grated palm sugar (jaggery) or soft brown sugar

SERVES 6

Grate the papaya, sprinkle with salt and leave for 30 minutes. Rinse well.

Cook the beans in a saucepan of boiling water for 3 minutes, or until tender. Drain, plunge into cold water, then drain again.

To make the dressing, combine all ingredients in a small bowl. Set aside.

Pound the garlic and chilli using a large mortar and pestle until crushed. Add the dried shrimp and pound until puréed. Add the papaya and snake beans and lightly pound for 1 minute. Add the tomato and pound briefly to bruise.

Combine the coriander with the papaya mixture and spoon onto serving plates. Pour the dressing over the top. Sprinkle with the peanuts and, if desired, sliced red chilli.

PREPARATION TIME: 25 MINUTES +   COOKING TIME: 5 MINUTES

WILD RICE SALAD

95 g (3¼ oz/½ cup) wild rice
250 ml (9 fl oz/1 cup) chicken stock
20 g (¾ oz) butter
100 g (3½ oz/½ cup) basmati rice
60 g (2¼ oz/½ cup) slivered almonds
1 tablespoon olive oil
2 back bacon slices, chopped
125 g (4½ oz) currants
30 g (1 oz) chopped flat-leaf (Italian) parsley
6 spring onions (scallions), thinly sliced
grated zest and juice of 1 lemon
olive oil, to drizzle
lemon wedges, to serve

SERVES 4

Put the wild rice and stock in a saucepan. Add the butter, bring to the boil, then cook, covered, over low heat for 1 hour. Drain.

Meanwhile, put the basmati rice in a separate saucepan with cold water and bring to the boil. Cook at a simmer for 12 minutes, then drain.

Mix the rices together in a bowl and allow to cool to room temperature.

Lightly toast the almonds in a dry frying pan for a few minutes, or until lightly golden. Heat the oil in the same pan and cook the bacon for 5 minutes, or until cooked. Remove from the pan and cool.

Combine the rice with the bacon, currants, almonds, parsley, spring onion and lemon zest and juice. Season, drizzle with oil and serve with lemon.

PREPARATION TIME: 20 MINUTES +   COOKING TIME: 1 HOUR

Green papaya salad

MIXED SEAFOOD SALAD

1.25 kg (2 lb 12 oz) large cooked prawns (shrimp)

12 cooked yabbies or crayfish

500 g (1 lb 2 oz) scallops

125 ml (4 fl oz/$\frac{1}{2}$ cup) dry white wine

pinch dried thyme

pinch dried tarragon or a bay leaf

400 g (14 oz) salmon, trout or firm white fish fillets, such as flake, hake or ling

6 hard-boiled eggs

150 g (5$\frac{1}{2}$ oz) mixed lettuce leaves

2 tablespoons chopped flat-leaf (Italian) parsley

2 ripe avocados, sliced

2 tablespoons lemon juice

VINAIGRETTE

125 ml (4 fl oz/$\frac{1}{2}$ cup) extra virgin olive oil

2 tablespoons white wine vinegar

1 teaspoon sugar

2 teaspoons dijon mustard

1 tablespoon chopped dill

GREEN GODDESS DRESSING

310 g (11 oz/1$\frac{1}{4}$ cups) whole-egg mayonnaise

4 tinned anchovy fillets, drained, and finely chopped

1 garlic clove, crushed

60 g (2$\frac{1}{4}$ oz/$\frac{1}{4}$ cup) sour cream

3 tablespoons chopped herbs, such as chives, parsley or dill

SERVES 8

Peel the prawns, leaving the tails intact. Gently pull out the dark vein from each prawn back, starting from the head end.

Cut down each side of the shell on the underside of each yabby with kitchen scissors, starting at the head and working towards the tail. Pull back the flap and remove the meat from each shell. Gently pull out the vein from each back and discard each shell.

Slice or pull off any vein, membrane or hard white muscle from the scallops.

Put 250 ml (9 fl oz/1 cup) water with the wine, herbs and a pinch each of salt and pepper in a saucepan. Bring to the boil, then reduce the heat and simmer for 5 minutes. Add the scallops and poach for a few minutes, or until they have just turned white, then remove with a slotted spoon and drain on a wire rack. Add the fish fillets to the gently simmering liquid. Poach until cooked and just tender, remove with a slotted spoon and drain on a wire rack. Break into large pieces.

Combine the prawns, yabbies, scallops and fish in a bowl. To make the vinaigrette, whisk together the oil, vinegar, sugar, mustard and dill, and season, to taste. Pour over the seafood, cover and refrigerate for 1 hour.

Peel and slice the eggs, reserving 2 yolks. Put half the lettuce leaves in a deep serving bowl. Arrange half the seafood over the lettuce, reserving the vinaigrette. Sprinkle with half the parsley, top with half the avocado, drizzle with half the lemon juice, then finish with half the sliced eggs, including the extra whites. Season with salt and pepper. Repeat the layers and season to taste. Drizzle with the reserved vinaigrette. Crumble the reserved egg yolks over the top. Serve with the green goddess dressing.

To make the green goddess dressing, mix all the ingredients in a bowl and season to taste.

PREPARATION TIME: 1 HOUR +   COOKING TIME: 20 MINUTES

CHICKPEA SALAD WITH CUMIN DRESSING

220 g (7³/4 oz/1 cup) dried chickpeas
3 tablespoons finely chopped flat-leaf
(Italian) parsley
1 small red onion, finely chopped
1 garlic clove, finely chopped
60 ml (2 fl oz/¹/4 cup) lemon juice
2 tablespoons olive oil
¹/2 teaspoon ground cumin
pinch cayenne pepper

SERVES 6

Soak the dried chickpeas in plenty of cold water for 8 hours, or overnight. Drain, put in a large saucepan, cover with water and bring to the boil over high heat. Reduce the heat to low and simmer for 1¹/2 hours, topping up with water to keep the chickpeas covered. Drain and cool.

Combine in a large bowl with the parsley, onion, garlic clove, lemon juice, olive oil, ground cumin, cayenne pepper and ¹/2 teaspoon each of salt and freshly ground black pepper. Toss well.

PREPARATION TIME: 20 MINUTES +   COOKING TIME: 1 HOUR 30 MINUTES

IDIYAPPAM

225 g (8 oz) rice sticks or dried rice
vermicelli
80 ml (2¹/2 fl oz/¹/3 cup) oil
50 g (1³/4 oz) cashew nuts
¹/2 onion, chopped
3 eggs
150 g (5¹/2 oz) fresh or frozen peas
10 curry leaves
2 carrots, grated
2 leeks, white part only, finely shredded
1 red capsicum (pepper), diced
2 tablespoons tomato sauce (ketchup)
1 tablespoon soy sauce

SERVES 4

Soak the rice sticks in cold water for about 30 minutes, then drain and put them in a saucepan of boiling water. Remove from the heat and leave in the pan for 3 minutes. Drain and refresh in cold water.

Heat 1 tablespoon of the oil in a frying pan and fry the cashews until golden. Remove, add the onion to the pan, fry until dark golden, then drain on paper towels.

Cook the eggs in boiling water for 10 minutes to hard-boil, then cool them immediately in cold water. When cold, peel and cut into wedges.

Cook the peas in boiling water until tender.

Heat the remaining oil in a frying pan and briefly fry the curry leaves. Add the carrot, leek and red capsicum and stir for 1 minute. Add the tomato sauce, soy sauce, 1 teaspoon salt and rice sticks and mix, stirring constantly to prevent the rice sticks from sticking to the pan. Serve on a platter and garnish with the peas, cashews, fried onion and egg wedges.

PREPARATION TIME: 10 MINUTES +   COOKING TIME: 20 MINUTES

Chickpea salad with cumin dressing

WILD RICE SALAD WITH CHINESE ROAST DUCK

200 g (7 oz/1 cup) wild rice
200 g (7 oz/1 cup) basmati or jasmine rice
16 thin asparagus spears, woody ends
trimmed, sliced
8 spring onions (scallions), thinly sliced
100 g (3½ oz) pecans, roughly chopped
100 g (3½ oz) dried cranberries
zest and juice of 1 orange
1 whole Chinese roast duck

DRESSING
125 ml (4 fl oz/½ cup) soy sauce
2 tablespoons sugar
1½ tablespoons balsamic vinegar
1½ tablespoons peanut oil
2 teaspoons sesame oil
2 teaspoons grated fresh ginger
2 small red chillies, finely chopped

SERVES 4–6

Put the wild rice in a saucepan of cold salted water, bring to the boil and cook for 30 minutes. Add the basmati or jasmine rice and continue to cook for a further 10 minutes, or until both rices are just cooked. Drain and refresh under cold water, then drain again and transfer to a large bowl.

Blanch the asparagus in a saucepan of boiling water, then drain and refresh under cold water. Add to the bowl with the rice.

Add the spring onion, pecans, dried cranberries and orange zest to the rice and mix together well.

Combine all the dressing ingredients and the orange juice in a screw-top jar and shake well.

Preheat the oven to 200°C (400°F/Gas 6). Remove the skin from the duck and break it into rough pieces. Shred the duck meat and add it to the salad. Put the skin on a baking tray and bake for 5 minutes, or until crispy. Drain on paper towel, then slice.

If necessary, shake the dressing again before pouring it over the salad. Toss to combine. Serve the salad in individual bowls, topped with pieces of crispy duck skin.

PREPARATION TIME: 15 MINUTES   COOKING TIME: 50 MINUTES

LENTIL SALAD

1 small onion
2 whole cloves
300 g (10½ oz/1½ cups) puy lentils or tiny blue-green lentils (see Note)
1 strip lemon zest
2 garlic cloves, peeled
1 bay leaf
2 teaspoons ground cumin
2 tablespoons red wine vinegar
60 ml (2 fl oz/¼ cup) olive oil
1 tablespoon lemon juice
2 tablespoons finely chopped mint
3 spring onions (scallions), thinly sliced

SERVES 4–6

Stud the onion with the cloves and put in a saucepan with the lentils, zest, garlic, bay leaf, 1 teaspoon of the cumin and 875 ml (28 fl oz/ 3½ cups) water. Bring to the boil and simmer gently over medium heat for 25–30 minutes, or until the lentils are tender. Drain off any excess liquid and discard the onion, zest and bay leaf. Reserve the garlic and finely chop.

Whisk together the vinegar, oil, lemon juice, garlic and remaining cumin. Stir the dressing through the lentils with the mint and spring onion. Season well, then leave for 30 minutes to allow the flavours to develop. Serve at room temperature.

PREPARATION TIME: 15 MINUTES +   COOKING TIME: 30 MINUTES

NOTE: Puy lentils are small green lentils, available from gourmet food stores.

FAST SPINACH SALAD

2 tablespoons olive oil
1 garlic clove, crushed
2 teaspoons white wine vinegar
100 g (3½ oz) mushrooms, thinly sliced
300 g (10½ oz) English spinach leaves, torn
2 hard-boiled eggs, sliced
100 g (3½ oz) feta cheese

SERVES 2–4

In a large bowl, mix together the olive oil, garlic, white wine vinegar and a little black pepper. Add the mushrooms and stir to coat well.

Put the spinach leaves in a salad bowl. Add mushrooms and dressing and the egg. Toss well. Crumble the feta cheese over the top.

PREPARATION TIME: 15 MINUTES   COOKING TIME: NIL

CHICKEN AND CHORIZO PAELLA

60 ml (2 fl oz/¼ cup) olive oil
1 large red capsicum (pepper), cut into 5 mm (¼ inch) strips
600 g (1 lb 5 oz) boneless, skinless chicken thighs, cut into 3 cm (1¼ inch) cubes
200 g (7 oz) chorizo, cut into 2 cm (¾ inch) slices
200 g (7 oz) mushrooms, thinly sliced
3 garlic cloves, crushed
1 tablespoon grated lemon zest
700 g (1 lb 9 oz) ripe tomatoes, roughly chopped
200 g (7 oz) green beans, trimmed and cut into 3 cm (1¼ inch) lengths
1 tablespoon chopped rosemary
2 tablespoons chopped flat-leaf (Italian) parsley
¼ teaspoon saffron threads dissolved in 60 ml (2 fl oz/¼ cup) hot water
440 g (15½ oz/2 cups) short-grain white rice
750 ml (26 fl oz/3 cups) hot chicken stock
6 lemon wedges, to serve

SERVES 6

Heat the olive oil in a paella pan or in a large, heavy-based, deep frying pan over medium heat. Add the red capsicum strips and cook, stirring, for about 6 minutes, or until softened, then remove from the pan.

Add the chicken to the pan and cook for 10 minutes, or until browned. Remove from the pan. Add the chorizo to the pan and cook for 5 minutes, or until golden. Remove from the pan. Add the mushrooms, garlic and lemon zest to the pan, and cook over medium heat for 5 minutes.

Stir in the tomato and capsicum, and cook for a further 5 minutes, or until the tomato is soft.

Add the beans, rosemary, parsley, saffron mixture, rice, chicken and chorizo. Stir briefly and add the stock. Do not stir at this point. Reduce the heat and simmer for 30 minutes. Remove from the heat, cover and leave to stand for 10 minutes. Serve with lemon wedges.

PREPARATION TIME: 30 MINUTES +   COOKING TIME: 1 HOUR 5 MINUTES

NOTE: Paella pans are available from specialist kitchenware shops.

PLATES AND NAPKINS

ROSETTAS

7 g (¹/₄ oz) dried yeast
1 teaspoon sugar
560 g (1 lb 4 oz/4¹/₂ cups) unbleached
plain (all-purpose) flour, sifted
50 g (1³/₄ oz) butter, softened
60 ml (2 fl oz/¹/₄ cup) olive oil
55 g (2 oz/¹/₄ cup) caster (superfine)
sugar
milk, to glaze
plain (all-purpose) flour, extra, to dust

MAKES 10

Lightly grease two baking trays. Put the yeast, sugar and 125 ml (4 fl oz/ ¹/₂ cup) warm water in a small bowl and stir well. Leave in a warm, draught-free place for 10 minutes, or until bubbles appear on the surface. The mixture should be frothy and slightly increased in volume. If your yeast doesn't foam it is dead, so you will have to discard it and start again.

Set aside 30 g (1 oz/¹/₄ cup) of the flour and put the rest in a large bowl with 1 teaspoon salt. Make a well in the centre. Add the yeast mixture, butter, oil, sugar and 315 ml (10³/₄ fl oz/1¹/₄ cups) warm water. Stir with a wooden spoon until the dough leaves the side of the bowl and forms a rough, sticky ball. Turn out onto a floured surface. Knead for 10 minutes, or until the dough is smooth and elastic. Add enough of the reserved flour, if necessary, to make a smooth dough. Put in a large, lightly oiled bowl and brush the surface with melted butter or oil. Cover with plastic wrap and leave in a warm place for 1 hour, or until well risen.

Punch down the dough, then knead for 1 minute. Divide into ten portions and shape each into a smooth ball. Place the balls 5 cm (2 inches) apart on the trays. Using a 3 cm (1¹/₄ inch) round cutter, press a 1 cm (¹/₂ inch) deep indent into the centre of each ball. With a sharp knife, score five evenly spaced, 1 cm (¹/₂ inch) deep cuts down the side of each roll. Cover with plastic wrap or a damp tea towel (dish towel) and leave in a warm place for 1 hour, or until well risen.

Preheat the oven to 180°C (350°F/Gas 4). Brush the rolls with milk and sift a fine layer of the extra flour over them. Bake for 25 minutes, or until golden. Rotate the trays in the oven if one tray is browning faster than the other. Allow to cool on a wire rack.

PREPARATION TIME: 40 MINUTES +   COOKING TIME: 25 MINUTES

NOTE: These are best eaten on the day of cooking, or they can be frozen for up to 1 month.

CHEESE AND SPINACH ROULADE BRUSCHETTA

1 baguette or crusty Italian loaf
2 tablespoons oil
500 g (1 lb 2 oz) English spinach
90 g (3¼ oz) cream cheese
90 g (3¼ oz) goat's cheese
3 tablespoons tinned pimiento, drained and finely chopped

MAKES ABOUT 24

Preheat the oven to 200°C (400°F/Gas 6). Cut the bread into 1 cm (½ inch) slices, brush with olive oil and grill (broil) until golden on both sides.

Remove the stalks from the spinach and put the leaves in a bowl. Cover with boiling water and leave for a couple of minutes, or until the leaves have wilted. Drain and leave to cool. Squeeze out the excess liquid and drain on crumpled paper towel.

Lay the spinach leaves flat, overlapping, on a piece of plastic wrap, to form a 20 x 25 cm (8 x 10 inch) rectangle. Beat the cheeses together until soft and smooth. Spread the cheese mixture evenly and carefully over the spinach. Top the cheese evenly with pimiento. Using the plastic wrap as a guide, roll up the spinach to enclose the cheese. Remove the plastic wrap and cut the log into thin slices using a sharp knife. Serve on the toast.

PREPARATION TIME: 30 MINUTES   COOKING TIME: 10 MINUTES

NOTES: The bread slices can be baked several days ahead and stored in an airtight container.

The roulade can be made a day ahead and stored, wrapped in plastic wrap, in the refrigerator. Assemble just before serving time.

SMOKED SALMON AND CAPER BRUSCHETTA

1 baguette or crusty Italian loaf
250 g (9 oz) cream cheese
2 tablespoons lemon juice
15 g (½ oz) snipped chives
100 g (3½ oz) smoked salmon, sliced
2 tablespoons baby capers, rinsed
2 dill sprigs, to garnish

MAKES ABOUT 24

Cut the bread into 1 cm (½ inch) slices, brush with olive oil and grill (broil) until golden on both sides.

Mix the cream cheese with the lemon juice and chives. Spread over the toast and top with small slices of smoked salmon and a few baby capers. Garnish with sprigs of dill before serving.

PREPARATION TIME: 20 MINUTES   COOKING TIME: 5 MINUTES

Cheese and spinach roulade bruschetta

OLIVE OIL BISCUITS WITH TOMATO FETA SALSA

7 g (¹/₄ oz) dried yeast or 15 g (¹/₂ oz)
fresh yeast
1 teaspoon sugar
185 g (6¹/₂ oz/1¹/₂ cups) plain
(all purpose) flour
225 g (8 oz/1¹/₂ cups) plain (all-purpose)
wholemeal (whole-wheat) flour
1 teaspoon ground cinnamon
1¹/₂ tablespoons sesame seeds, toasted
125 ml (4 fl oz/¹/₂ cup) olive oil

TOMATO FETA SALSA
4 ripe tomatoes, diced
160 g (5³/₄ oz) feta cheese, crumbled
80 ml (2¹/₂ fl oz/¹/₃ cup) extra virgin
olive oil
2 tablespoons red wine vinegar
1 teaspoon dried oregano

MAKES ABOUT 45

Mix the yeast, sugar, 2 tablespoons of the plain flour and 60 ml (2 fl oz/ ¹/₄ cup) warm water in a bowl. Cover with plastic wrap and leave in a warm place for 10 minutes, or until frothy.

Sift the remaining flours and cinnamon into a large bowl, return the husks to the bowl and stir through the sesame seeds and ¹/₂ teaspoon salt. Pour in the oil and rub it in by lifting the flour mixture onto one hand and lightly rubbing the other hand over the top. Make a well in the centre and add the yeast mixture and about 60 ml (2 fl oz/¹/₄ cup) warm water, or enough to mix to a soft but not sticky dough. Knead on a floured surface for about 2 minutes, or until smooth and elastic. Put in a lightly oiled bowl, turning the dough to coat in the oil. Cover loosely with plastic wrap and leave in a warm place for 45–60 minutes, or until doubled in bulk.

Preheat the oven to 200°C (400°F/Gas 6). Lightly grease a baking tray. Punch down the dough to expel the air, divide it into three portions and roll each on a lightly floured surface into a long sausage shape about 30 cm (12 inches) long. Put the first roll on the baking tray. Cut through almost to the base of the roll at 2 cm (³/₄ inch) intervals with a serrated knife (about 15 portions). Repeat with the remaining rolls.

Cover with a tea towel (dish towel) and leave in a warm place for 30 minutes, or until well risen. Bake for 30 minutes, or until browned underneath and the rolls sound hollow when tapped. Reduce the oven temperature to 120°C (250°F/ Gas ¹/₂). Cool the rolls on the tray for 5 minutes. Transfer each roll to a cutting board and cut through the markings. Place, cut side up, on two baking trays. Bake for 30 minutes, or until the tops feel dry. Turn each biscuit and bake for a further 30 minutes, or until completely dry and crisp. Allow to cool. Store in an airtight container for up to 3 weeks.

Dunk each biscuit quickly into cold water and place on a tray. Top with the combined tomato and feta. Drizzle with the combined oil and vinegar and sprinkle with oregano. Season.

PREPARATION TIME: 30 MINUTES + COOKING TIME: 1 HOUR 30 MINUTES

SPANISH TORTILLA

125 ml (4 fl oz/½ cup) olive oil
2 large all-purpose potatoes, peeled and
cut into 5 mm (¼ inch) slices
2 large onions, sliced
3 eggs

MAKES 16 WEDGES

Heat the oil in a 20 cm (8 inch) diameter deep non-stick frying pan with a lid. Place alternate layers of potato and onion in the pan, cover and cook for 8 minutes over low heat. Using tongs, turn the layers in sections (it doesn't matter if they break up). Cover and cook for 8 minutes, without allowing the potato to colour.

Put a strainer over a bowl and drain the potato mixture, reserving 1 tablespoon of the oil.

Put the eggs and a little salt and pepper in a bowl and whisk to combine. Add the potato mixture, pressing down with the back of a spoon to completely cover with the egg.

Heat the reserved oil in the same frying pan over high heat. Pour in the egg mixture, pressing down to even it out. Reduce the heat to low, cover with a lid and cook for 12 minutes, or until set. Gently shake the pan to ensure the tortilla is not sticking. Leave for 5 minutes, then invert onto a plate. Cut into wedges. Serve at room temperature.

PREPARATION TIME: 20 MINUTES +   COOKING TIME: 30 MINUTES

ROCKET AND FETA BRUSCHETTA

1 baguette or crusty Italian loaf
90 g (3¼ oz) rocket (arugula) leaves
200 g (7 oz) feta cheese, crumbled
2 teaspoons finely grated orange zest
2 tablespoons olive oil
6 prosciutto slices

MAKES ABOUT 30

Cut the bread into 1 cm (½ inch) slices, brush with olive oil and grill (broil) until golden on both sides.

Arrange the rocket leaves over each piece. Toss the feta with the orange zest and olive oil. Spoon 2 teaspoons of the mixture over the rocket on each bruschetta.

Grill (broil) the prosciutto until crispy, then crumble over the bruschetta.

PREPARATION TIME: 10 MINUTES   COOKING TIME: 10 MINUTES

CROSTINI WITH CAPSICUM ROULADE

2 red capsicums (peppers)
2 yellow capsicums (peppers)
8 English spinach leaves
1 tablespoon chopped flat-leaf (Italian) parsley
1 small baguette
2 tablespoons olive oil
shaved parmesan cheese, to garnish

MAKES ABOUT 20

Preheat the grill (broiler). Cut each capsicum in half and grill, skin side up, until the skin is black and blistered. Cool in a plastic bag, then peel.

Remove the stalks from the spinach and put the leaves in a bowl. Cover with boiling water and set aside for a couple of minutes until the leaves have wilted. Drain and cool. Squeeze out the excess water and spread the leaves out. Pat dry with paper towels.

Lay two sheets of overlapping plastic wrap on a flat surface. Flatten out the red capsicum to form a rectangle, overlapping the ends. Lay the spinach leaves over the capsicum to make a second layer. Put the flattened yellow capsicum on top to make a third layer, making sure there are no gaps, and overlapping the ends. Sprinkle with the parsley. Using the plastic wrap to assist, roll up the capsicum tightly lengthways, sealing the ends. Wrap tightly in foil, twist the ends firmly and chill for 3 hours.

Preheat the oven to 200°C (400°F/Gas 6). Cut the baguette stick into 1 cm ($^1/_2$ inch) slices. Put on a baking tray, lightly brush with olive oil, sprinkle with salt and bake for 5–10 minutes, or until golden.

Remove the plastic wrap, cut the roulade into 1.5 cm ($^5/_8$ inch) thick slices and place on the crostini. Drizzle with oil. Garnish with parmesan.

PREPARATION TIME: 30 MINUTES +   COOKING TIME: 10 MINUTES

NOTE: The topping and the bread can be prepared separately up to 6 hours in advance. However, don't top the bread any earlier than 30 minutes before serving as it may go soft.

CHILLI POLENTA CAKE

165 g (5³/4 oz/1¹/3 cups) plain (all purpose) flour
1¹/2 teaspoons baking powder
185 g (6¹/2 oz/1¹/4 cups) polenta
125 g (4¹/2 oz/1 cup) grated cheddar cheese
250 g (9 oz/1 cup) plain yoghurt
125 ml (4 fl oz/¹/2 cup) milk
2 eggs
80 g (2³/4 oz/¹/2 cup) chopped red capsicum (pepper)
2 teaspoons chopped chilli
60 g (2¹/4 oz) unsalted butter

MAKES ONE 20 CM (8 INCH) CAKE

Preheat the oven to 200°C (400°F/Gas 6). Sift the flour, baking powder and 1 teaspoon salt into a large bowl. Mix in the polenta and cheese.

In a separate bowl, whisk together the yoghurt, milk, eggs, red capsicum and chilli.

Heat a 20 cm (8 inch) ovenproof frying pan and melt the butter. Stir the butter into the yoghurt mixture. Pour all the liquid ingredients into the dry ingredients. Mix well.

Pour into the frying pan. Cook in the oven for 25–30 minutes, or until a skewer inserted in the centre comes out clean.

PREPARATION TIME: 25 MINUTES   COOKING TIME: 30 MINUTES

CHILLI AND CORIANDER FRITTATA

3 all-purpose potatoes, cut into small cubes
2 banana chillies
2 tablespoons olive oil
1 onion, finely chopped
1 small red chilli, finely chopped
1 tablespoon chopped coriander (cilantro) leaves
5 eggs, beaten

SERVES 6

Cook the potatoes in a large saucepan of boiling water until just tender. Drain well.

Remove the seeds from the banana chillies and slice the flesh. Heat half the oil in a non-stick frying pan. Cook the banana chilli over medium heat for 2 minutes, or until softened. Remove from the pan and set aside. Heat the remaining oil in the pan. Add the onion and red chilli. Cook over medium heat for 3 minutes, or until soft. Add the potato and toss to combine. Remove from the pan and set aside.

Return half the banana chilli to the pan and sprinkle with the coriander. Layer half the potato mixture, banana chilli, and remaining potato mixture.

Pour the eggs into the pan. Cook over medium–low heat for 8 minutes, or until the eggs are almost cooked through, then put under a hot grill (broiler) for 4 minutes to cook the top. Invert the frittata onto a plate. Allow to cool, then cut into wedges. Serve cold.

PREPARATION TIME: 25 MINUTES   COOKING TIME: 30 MINUTES

Chilli polenta cake

VEGETABLE FRITTATA WITH HUMMUS AND BLACK OLIVES

HUMMUS
425 g (15 oz) tinned chickpeas, drained
2 garlic cloves, crushed
80 ml (2¹/₂ fl oz/¹/₃ cup) lemon juice
2 tablespoons plain yoghurt

2 large red capsicums (peppers)
600 g (1 lb 5 oz) orange sweet potato
500 g (1 lb 2 oz) eggplant (aubergine)
80 ml (2¹/₂ fl oz/¹/₃ cup) olive oil
2 leeks, thinly sliced
2 garlic cloves, crushed
250 g (9 oz) zucchini (courgettes),
thinly sliced
8 eggs, lightly beaten
2 tablespoons finely chopped basil
125 g (4¹/₂ oz) parmesan cheese, grated
60 g (2¹/₄ oz) black olives, pitted and
halved, to serve

MAKES 30 SQUARES

To make the hummus, in a food processor, purée the chickpeas, garlic, lemon juice, yoghurt and a pinch of black pepper.

Preheat the grill (broiler). Cut the capsicums into quarters and grill, skin side up, until the skin is black and blistered. Cool in a plastic bag, then peel.

Cut the sweet potato into 1 cm (¹/₂ inch) thick slices and cook until just tender, then drain.

Cut the eggplant into 1 cm (¹/₂ inch) slices. Heat 1 tablespoon of the oil in a 23 cm (9 inch) round, deep frying pan and stir the leek and garlic over medium heat for 1 minute, or until soft. Add the zucchini and cook for another 2 minutes. Remove from the pan and set aside.

Heat the remaining oil in the same frying pan and cook the eggplant slices, in batches, for 1 minute each side, or until golden. Line the base of the pan with half the eggplant and spread the leek over the top. Cover with the roasted capsicum, remaining eggplant and sweet potato.

Combine the eggs, basil, parmesan and some black pepper in a jug, pour over the vegetables and cook over low heat for 15 minutes, or until almost cooked. Put the frying pan under a preheated grill (broiler) for 2-3 minutes, or until the frittata is golden and cooked. Cool for 10 minutes before inverting onto a cutting board. Trim the edges and cut into 30 squares. Top with hummus and olives. Serve at room temperature.

PREPARATION TIME: 30 MINUTES +   COOKING TIME: 35 MINUTES

HERBED GOAT'S CHEESE

200 g (7 oz) vine leaves in brine
3 teaspoons green or pink peppercorns,
drained and chopped
1 tablespoon chopped marjoram
3 x 100 g (3½ oz) rounds soft goat's
cheese

SERVES 6–8

Place the vine leaves in a heatproof bowl and cover with hot water to rinse away the brine. Drain well and pat dry with paper towels.

Combine the peppercorns and marjoram in a shallow bowl. Toss the goat's cheese in the mixture until the sides are well coated.

Arrange a few vine leaves, shiny side down, on a work surface. Wrap each goat's cheese round in a few layers of vine leaves.

Cook the cheese on a barbecue hotplate or under a hot grill (broiler) for 3 minutes each side, or until the outside leaves are charred. Transfer to a plate and allow to cool to room temperature. (The cheese is too soft to serve when hot, but will firm as it cools.) Use scissors to cut away the vine leaves and serve the cheese with the rye bread.

PREPARATION TIME: 20 MINUTES   COOKING TIME: 10 MINUTES

NOTE: The cheese can be wrapped in the vine leaves a few hours ahead.

MINI CRAB AND LIME QUICHES

2 sheets frozen puff pastry, thawed
2 eggs
185 ml (6 fl oz/¾ cup) coconut cream
finely grated zest of 1 small lime
2 teaspoons lime juice
200 g (7 oz) tinned crabmeat, drained
1 tablespoon snipped chives
white pepper, to season

MAKES 18

Preheat the oven to 210°C (415°F/Gas 6–7). Using two 12-hole round-based patty pans or mini muffin tins, lightly grease 18 of the holes. Cut 18 rounds of pastry, using an 8 cm (3 inch) cutter.

Beat the eggs lightly in a small bowl and add the remaining ingredients. Season with salt and white pepper. Spoon about 1 tablespoon of the filling into each pastry case.

Bake for 20 minutes, or until golden. The quiches will rise during cooking, then deflate slightly. Serve at room temperature.

PREPARATION TIME: 15 MINUTES   COOKING TIME: 20 MINUTES

Herbed goat's cheese

KIBBEH

235 g (8½ oz/1⅓ cups) fine burghul
(bulgur)
150 g (5½ oz) lean lamb, chopped
1 onion, grated
2 tablespoons plain (all-purpose) flour
1 teaspoon ground allspice

FILLING
2 teaspoons olive oil
1 small onion, finely chopped
100 g (3½ oz) lean minced (ground) lamb
½ teaspoon ground allspice
½ teaspoon ground cinnamon
80 ml (2½ fl oz/⅓ cup) beef stock
2 tablespoons pine nuts
2 tablespoons chopped mint

MAKES 15

Put the burghul in a large bowl, cover with boiling water and leave for 5 minutes. Drain in a colander, pressing well to remove the water. Spread on paper towels to absorb the remaining moisture.

Process the burghul, lamb, onion, flour and allspice until a fine paste forms. Season well, then refrigerate for 1 hour.

To make the filling, heat the oil in a frying pan, add the onion and cook over low heat for 3 minutes, or until soft. Add the lamb, allspice and cinnamon, and stir over high heat for 3 minutes. Add the stock and cook, partially covered, over low heat for 6 minutes, or until the lamb is soft. Roughly chop the pine nuts and stir in with the mint. Season, then transfer to a bowl and allow to cool.

Shape 2 tablespoons of the burghul mixture into a sausage shape 6 cm (2½ inches) long. Dip your hands in cold water and, with your finger, make a long hole through the centre and gently work your finger around to make a shell. Fill with 2 teaspoons of the filling and seal, moulding it into a torpedo shape. Smooth over any cracks with your fingers. Put on a foil-lined tray and repeat with the remaining ingredients to make 15 kibbeh. Refrigerate, uncovered, for 1 hour.

Fill a deep heavy-based frying pan one-third full of oil and heat the oil to 180°C (350°F), or until a cube of bread dropped into the oil turns golden brown in 15 seconds. Deep-fry the kibbeh in batches for 2–3 minutes, or until well browned. Drain on crumpled paper towels.

PREPARATION TIME: 45 MINUTES +   COOKING TIME: 25 MINUTES

LAYERED LAMB AND BURGHUL

350 g (12 oz/2 cups) burghul (bulgur)
400 g (14 oz) minced (ground) lamb
1 large onion, finely chopped
1 tablespoon ground cumin
1 teaspoon ground allspice
olive oil, for brushing

FILLING
1 tablespoon olive oil, plus extra
for brushing
1 onion, finely chopped
1 teaspoon ground cinnamon
1 tablespoon ground cumin
500 g (1 lb 2 oz) minced (ground) lamb
80 g (2³/4 oz/¹/2 cup) raisins
100 g (3¹/2 oz) pine nuts, toasted
plain yoghurt, to serve

SERVES 4–6

Soak the burghul in cold water for 30 minutes, then drain and squeeze out excess water. Put the lamb, onion, cumin, allspice and some salt and pepper in a food processor, and process until combined. Add the burghul and process to a paste. Refrigerate until needed. Preheat the oven to 180°C (350°F/Gas 4). Lightly grease a 20 x 30 cm (8 x 12 inch) baking dish.

To make the filling, heat the oil in a large frying pan over medium heat and cook the onion for 5 minutes, or until softened. Add the cinnamon and cumin and stir for 1 minute, or until fragrant. Add the lamb, stirring to break up any lumps, and cook for 5 minutes, or until the meat is brown. Stir in the raisins and nuts and season, to taste.

Press half the burghul mixture into the base of the tin, smoothing the surface with wet hands. Spread the filling over the top, then cover with the remaining burghul, again smoothing the top.

Score a diamond pattern in the top of the mixture with a knife and brush with olive oil. Bake for 40 minutes, or until the top is brown. Cool for 10 minutes before cutting into diamond shapes. Serve with plain yoghurt.

PREPARATION TIME: 30 MINUTES +   COOKING TIME: 55 MINUTES

TROUT, FETTUCINE AND FENNEL FRITTATA

250 g (9 oz) whole smoked trout
200 g (7 oz) fettucine
250 ml (9 fl oz/1 cup) milk
125 ml (4 fl oz/¹/2 cup) pouring (whipping) cream
4 eggs
pinch freshly grated nutmeg
40 g (1¹/2 oz) thinly sliced fennel
4 spring onions (scallions), sliced
85 g (3 oz/²/3 cup) grated cheddar cheese

SERVES 4

Preheat the oven to 180°C (350°F/Gas 4). Lightly grease a 23 cm (9 inch) flan dish. Remove and discard the skin and bones from the trout.

Cook the fettucine in a large saucepan of rapidly boiling salted water until *al dente*. Drain.

Combine the milk, cream, eggs and nutmeg in a large bowl and whisk until smooth. Season to taste. Add the trout, fettucine, fennel and spring onion and toss to distribute evenly. Pour into the prepared dish and sprinkle with the cheese. Bake for about 1 hour, or until set.

PREPARATION TIME: 20 MINUTES   COOKING TIME: 1 HOUR 10 MINUTES

Layered lamb and burghul

BACON AND EGG PIE

2 tablespoons oil
4 bacon slices, chopped
250 g (9 oz) frozen shortcrust (pie) pastry, thawed
250 g (9 oz) block frozen ready-made puff pastry, thawed
5 eggs, beaten
60 ml (2 fl oz/¼ cup) pouring (whipping) cream
1 egg, beaten, extra

SERVES 4–6

Lightly grease a 20 cm (8 inch) loose-based pie tin. Heat the oil in a frying pan. Add the bacon and cook over medium heat for a few minutes, or until lightly browned. Drain on paper towels and allow to cool slightly.

Roll out the shortcrust pastry between two sheets of baking paper until slightly larger than the tin. Put in the tin and roll a rolling pin over the tin to trim off any excess pastry. Refrigerate for 20 minutes. Preheat the oven to 210°C (415°F/Gas 6–7).

Line the pastry shell with a piece of baking paper and pour in some baking beads or uncooked rice. Bake for 10 minutes, then remove the paper and beads and cook for a further 10 minutes, or until the pastry is dry and golden. Allow to cool.

Roll out the puff pastry between two sheets of baking paper to a circle large enough to cover the top of the pie. Arrange the bacon over the cooled pastry base and pour the combined egg and cream over the top. Cover the pie with the puff pastry and press on firmly to seal. Trim the pastry edges and decorate the top with shapes cut from the pastry scraps. Brush with the extra egg and bake for 30–35 minutes, or until the pastry is puffed and golden. Serve at room temperature.

PREPARATION TIME: 20 MINUTES +   COOKING TIME: 1 HOUR

NOTE: Bacon and egg pie can be made a day ahead and refrigerated overnight. Allow to come to room temperature before serving.

GOAT'S CHEESE GALETTE

PASTRY

125 g (4¹/2 oz/1 cup) plain (all-purpose) flour

60 ml (2 fl oz/¹/4 cup) olive oil

FILLING

1 tablespoon olive oil

2 onions, thinly sliced

1 teaspoon thyme

125 g (4¹/2 oz) ricotta cheese

100 g (3¹/2 oz) goat's cheese

2 tablespoons pitted niçoise olives

1 egg, beaten

60 ml (2 fl oz/¹/4 cup) pouring (whipping) cream

SERVES 6

To make the pastry, sift the flour and a pinch of salt into a bowl and make a well in the centre. Add the olive oil and mix with a flat-bladed knife until crumbly. Gradually add 60–80 ml (2–2¹/2 fl oz/¹/4–¹/3 cup) water until the mixture comes together. Remove and pat together to form a disc. Refrigerate for 30 minutes.

Meanwhile, to make the filling, heat the oil in a frying pan. Add the onion, cover and cook for 30 minutes. Season and stir in half the thyme. Cool.

Preheat the oven to 180°C (350°F/Gas 4). Lightly flour the workbench and roll out the pastry to a 30 cm (12 inch) circle. Then put on a heated baking tray. Evenly spread the onion over the pastry, leaving a 2 cm (³/4 inch) border. Sprinkle the ricotta and goat's cheese evenly over the onion. Put the olives over the cheeses, then sprinkle with the remaining thyme. Fold the pastry border in to the edge of the filling, pleating as you go.

Combine the egg and cream, then pour over the filling. Bake in the lower half of the oven for 45 minutes, or until the pastry is golden.

PREPARATION TIME: 20 MINUTES +   COOKING TIME: 1 HOUR 15 MINUTES

MEDITERRANEAN SQUARES

1 red onion

3 tablespoons pitted black olives

1 red capsicum (pepper)

1 green capsicum (pepper)

2 tablespoons basil

3 teaspoons balsamic vinegar

2 garlic cloves, crushed

60 ml (2 fl oz/¹/4 cup) oil

3 garlic cloves, crushed, extra

30 x 40 cm (12 x 16 inch) piece focaccia

90 g (3¹/4 oz/³/4 cup) grated cheddar cheese

MAKES ABOUT 20

Preheat the oven to 180°C (350°F/Gas 4) and line a baking tray with foil. Slice the onion and olives. Cut the capsicums in half and cut the remaining flesh into thin strips. Finely shred the basil leaves.

Combine the onion, olives, capsicums, basil, vinegar and garlic in a bowl. Mix well, then cover and set aside.

Combine the oil and extra garlic in a small bowl. Using a serrated knife, split the focaccia through the centre. Brush the focaccia halves with the combined oil and garlic. Arrange the combined olive and capsicum filling evenly over the bottom half of the focaccia. Sprinkle with the cheese and top with the remaining piece of focaccia. Put on the baking tray and bake for 15 minutes, or until the cheese melts. Cut into squares to serve.

PREPARATION TIME: 15 MINUTES   COOKING TIME: 15 MINUTES

RAISED PORK PIE

1.2 kg (2 lb 10 oz) minced (ground) pork
100 g (3^1/$_2$ oz/^{2}/$_3$ cup) pistachio nuts,
shelled and chopped
2 green apples, peeled and
finely chopped
6 sage leaves, finely chopped
500 g (1 lb 2 oz/4 cups) plain (all-purpose)
flour
150 g (5^1/$_2$ oz) lard
2 eggs, beaten
1 egg yolk
200 ml (7 fl oz) vegetable stock
200 ml (7 fl oz) unsweetened apple juice
2 teaspoons powdered gelatine

SERVES 8

Preheat the oven to 200°C (400°F/Gas 6). Combine the pork, pistachio nuts, apple and sage leaves in a bowl. Mix well and season. Cover and refrigerate until ready to use. Wrap plastic wrap around a 6 cm (2^1/$_2$ inch) high, 20 cm (8 inch) diameter round straight-sided tin, then turn the tin over, and grease the outside base and side of the tin.

Sift the flour and 1 teaspoon salt into a bowl and make a well in the centre. Put the lard in a saucepan with 210 ml (7^1/$_2$ fl oz) water, bring to the boil and add to the flour with the beaten eggs. Mix with a wooden spoon until combined, then turn out onto a work surface and bring the mixture together to form a smooth dough. Unlike any other kind of pastry, this hot water pastry must be kept warm. Cover with a cloth and leave in a warm place for 10 minutes until cool enough to handle.

When the pastry is just warm, set aside one-third — do not refrigerate. Roll the remainder into a circle large enough to just cover the outside of the tin. Lift onto a rolling pin and place over the tin, working fast before the pastry sets. Refrigerate until the pastry hardens. Carefully pull out the tin and remove the plastic wrap. Attach a paper collar made of two layers of greased baking paper around the outside of the pastry so it fits snugly. Secure with string or a paper clip at the top and bottom. Fill the pie with the pork mixture, then roll out the remaining pastry to form a lid. Attach it to the base with some water, pressing or crimping it to make it look neat. Cut a small hole in the top.

Put the pie on a baking tray. Bake for 40 minutes and check the pastry top. If it is still pale, bake for a further 10 minutes, then remove the paper. Brush with egg yolk mixed with 1 tablespoon water and bake for 15 minutes, or until the sides are brown. Remove from the oven and allow to cool completely.

Bring the stock and half the apple juice to the boil. Sprinkle the gelatine over the surface of the remaining apple juice in a measuring cup and leave to go spongy, then pour into the stock and mix until the gelatine dissolves. Put a small funnel (piping nozzles work well) in the hole of the pie and pour in a little of the gelatine mixture, leave to settle and then pour in some more until the pie is full. Fill the pie completely so there will be no gaps when the gelatine sets. Refrigerate overnight.

PREPARATION TIME: 50 MINUTES + COOKING TIME: 1 HOUR 10 MINUTES

BROWN RICE TART WITH FRESH TOMATO FILLING

RICE CRUST
200 g (7 oz/1 cup) brown rice
60 g (2¼ oz/½ cup) grated cheddar
cheese
1 egg, lightly beaten

FRESH TOMATO FILLING
6 roma (plum) tomatoes, halved
6 garlic cloves, unpeeled
1 tablespoon olive oil
8 lemon thyme sprigs
50 g (1¾ oz) goat's cheese, crumbled
3 eggs, beaten
60 ml (2 fl oz/¼ cup) milk

SERVES 6

To make the rice crust, cook the rice in a saucepan of boiling water for 35 minutes. Drain and set aside. Preheat the oven to 200°C (400°F/Gas 6).

Put the rice, cheese and egg into a bowl and mix until well combined. Spread the mixture over the base and sides of a lightly greased 25 cm (10 inch) flan tin or quiche dish and bake for 15 minutes.

To make the fresh tomato filling, put the tomatoes, cut side up, and garlic on a non-stick baking tray. Brush with oil and sprinkle with pepper. Bake for 30 minutes. Remove from the oven. Cool slightly. Remove the skins from the garlic. Reduce the oven to 180°C (350°F/Gas 4). Arrange the tomato halves, garlic, lemon thyme and goat's cheese over the rice crust.

Put the beaten eggs and milk in a bowl and whisk to combine. Pour over the tomatoes. Bake for 1 hour, or until set.

PREPARATION TIME: 25 MINUTES   COOKING TIME: 2 HOURS 20 MINUTES

SPINACH CROQUETTES

285 g (10 oz/1½ cups) short-grain rice
250 g (9 oz) feta cheese, crumbled
25 g (1 oz/¼ cup) freshly grated parmesan
cheese
2 eggs, beaten
1 garlic clove, crushed
2 teaspoons grated lemon zest
40 g (1½ oz/⅓ cup) chopped spring
onions (scallions)
250 g (9 oz) packet frozen spinach,
thawed, squeezed of excess moisture
1 tablespoon chopped dill
200 g (7 oz/2 cups) dry breadcrumbs
2 eggs, beaten, extra
oil, for deep-frying

MAKES 18

Cook the rice in a large saucepan of boiling water until just tender. Drain, then rinse under cold water, then drain again. Combine the rice, cheeses, egg, garlic, lemon zest, spring onion, spinach and dill in a bowl. Using wet hands, divide the mixture into 18 portions. Roll each portion into even-sized sausage shapes. Put on a tray and refrigerate for 30 minutes.

Spread the breadcrumbs on a sheet of greaseproof paper. Dip the croquettes into the extra beaten egg. Coat with the breadcrumbs and shake off the excess. Refrigerate for a further 30 minutes.

Fill a deep heavy-based frying pan one-third full of oil and heat to 180°C (350°F), or until a spoonful of the batter dropped into the oil turns golden brown in 15 seconds. Lower batches of croquettes into the oil with tongs or a slotted spoon. Cook for 2–3 minutes, or until golden and cooked through. Drain on paper towel. Repeat with the remaining croquettes. Serve cold with plain yoghurt.

PREPARATION TIME: 50 MINUTES +   COOKING TIME: 25 MINUTES

Brown rice tart with fresh tomato filling

DUTCH-STYLE BEEF AND RICE CROQUETTES

BÉCHAMEL SAUCE
20 g (³/₄ oz) butter
30 g (1 oz/¹/₄ cup) plain (all-purpose) flour
170 ml (5¹/₂ fl oz/²/₃ cup) milk
pinch freshly grated nutmeg

10 g (¹/₄ oz) butter
75 g (2¹/₂ oz/¹/₃ cup) arborio rice
410 ml (14 fl oz/1²/₃ cups) chicken stock
2 tablespoons olive oil
1 onion, finely chopped
2 garlic cloves, crushed
500 g (1 lb 2 oz) lean minced (ground) beef
100 ml (3¹/₂ fl oz) chicken stock, extra
1 tablespoon tomato paste (concentrated purée)
1 tablespoon worcestershire sauce
50 g (1³/₄ oz) gingernut biscuits, crushed (see Note)
2 tablespoons chopped flat-leaf (Italian) parsley
75 g (2¹/₂ oz/³/₄ cup) dry breadcrumbs
oil, for deep-frying

MAKES 12

To make the béchamel sauce, melt the butter in a small saucepan over medium heat. Stir in the flour and cook for 1 minute, or until foaming. Remove from the heat and gradually stir in the milk, beating well after each addition. After the last of the milk has been added, add the nutmeg and some salt and pepper. Return to the heat and stir constantly until the sauce boils and thickens. Set aside to cool.

Melt the butter in a saucepan. Add the rice and stir to coat. Gradually stir in the stock and continue stirring until it has come to the boil. Reduce the heat and simmer for about 20 minutes, or until the rice is very tender and all the stock has been absorbed.

Heat the oil in a large frying pan and cook the onion and garlic over low heat for about 5 minutes, or until softened but not browned. Add the beef and cook for 8 minutes, or until browned. Stir in the extra stock, tomato paste, worcestershire sauce, crushed gingernut biscuits and parsley. Simmer, covered, for 20 minutes. If there is still some liquid left after this time, take the lid off and cook over high heat to reduce it.

Combine the béchamel, rice and beef and season well. Cool slightly, then refrigerate for 1 hour. Divide the mixture into twelve parts and roll each into a log approximately 7 cm (2³/₄ inches) long and 3 cm (1¹/₄ inches) in diameter. The mixture will be soft, but manageable. Roll the logs in breadcrumbs to coat all over and put on a plate in a single layer. Cover with plastic wrap and refrigerate overnight.

Fill a large saucepan one-third full of oil and heat to 180°C (350°F), or until a spoonful of the batter dropped into the oil turns golden brown in 15 seconds. Cook the croquettes, a few at a time, turning them with tongs to give an evenly golden brown surface. Drain on crumpled paper towels.

PREPARATION TIME: 30 MINUTES +   COOKING TIME: 1 HOUR 30 MINUTES

NOTE: If gingernut biscuits are unavailable, crush 50 g (1³/₄ oz) wheatmeal biscuits with ¹/₂ teaspoon ground ginger.

FRIED CIGAR PASTRIES

16 fresh asparagus spears
2 tablespoons finely grated lemon zest
2 sheets frozen puff pastry, thawed
1 egg yolk
1 tablespoon sesame seeds

MAKES 16

Preheat the oven to 200°C (400°F/Gas 6). Add the asparagus to a large saucepan of lightly salted boiling water. Simmer for about 3 minutes, then drain and refresh under cold running water. Trim to 10 cm (4 inch) lengths.

Combine 1/2 teaspoon each of salt and black pepper and the lemon zest in a shallow dish and roll each asparagus spear in this mixture.

Cut the puff pastry sheets into 6 x 12 cm (2 1/2 x 5 inch) rectangles and put one asparagus spear on each piece of pastry. In a bowl, combine the egg yolk with 2 teaspoons water and brush some on the sides and ends of the pastry. Roll the pastry up like a parcel, enclosing the sides so that the asparagus is completely sealed in. Press the joins of the pastry with a fork.

Place the parcels on lightly greased baking trays. Brush with the remaining egg and sprinkle with sesame seeds. Bake for 15–20 minutes, or until golden. Served cold with tzatziki.

PREPARATION TIME: 20 MINUTES   COOKING TIME: 25 MINUTES

VEGETABLE PASTIES

1 potato
1 carrot
1 parsnip
100 g (3 1/2 oz) pumpkin (winter squash)
2 teaspoons oil
1 onion, finely chopped
125 ml (4 fl oz/1/2 cup) vegetable stock
50 g (1 3/4 oz/1/3 cup) fresh or frozen peas
1 tablespoon finely chopped flat-leaf (Italian) parsley
3 sheets frozen puff pastry, thawed
1 egg, lightly beaten
tomato sauce (ketchup), to serve

MAKES 12

Preheat the oven to 210°C (415°F/Gas 6-7). Lightly grease a baking tray. Peel and cut the potato, carrot, parsnip and pumpkin into 1 cm (1/2 inch) cubes.

Heat the oil in a frying pan and cook the onion over medium heat for 2 minutes, or until soft. Add the potato, carrot, parsnip, pumpkin and stock, then bring to the boil. Reduce the heat and simmer for 10 minutes, stirring occasionally, until the vegetables are soft and the liquid has evaporated. Stir in the peas and parsley and allow to cool.

Using a plate as a guide, cut four 12 cm (5 inch) circles from each sheet of pastry. Put 1 level tablespoon of mixture onto each round, brush the edges of pastry with water and fold the pastry over so the edges meet. Crimp the edges together to seal. Brush with beaten egg and place on the tray. Bake for 25 minutes, or until puffed and golden. Serve with tomato sauce.

PREPARATION TIME: 40 MINUTES   COOKING TIME: 50 MINUTES

CHIPOLATA SAUSAGES WITH HORSERADISH CREAM

2 tablespoons virgin olive oil
2 red onions, cut into thin wedges
2 tablespoons dark brown sugar
3 teaspoons balsamic vinegar
100 g (3½ oz) cream cheese
1 tablespoon horseradish cream
12 chipolata sausages
12 par-baked mini bread rolls
100 g (3½ oz) rocket (arugula) leaves,
stalks removed

MAKES 12

Preheat the oven to 220°C (425°F/Gas 7). Heat 1½ tablespoons olive oil in a small saucepan. Add the onion and 1½ tablespoons water. Cover and cook over medium heat for about 10 minutes, stirring occasionally, until the onion is soft and starting to brown. Stir in the sugar and vinegar and cook, uncovered, for 3 minutes, or until thick. Season and keep warm.

Meanwhile, combine the cream cheese and horseradish cream in a small bowl and mix until smooth.

Heat the remaining oil in a large frying pan and cook the sausages in batches over medium–low heat for 6–8 minutes, or until brown and cooked. Remove and drain on crumpled paper towels.

Meanwhile, heat the bread rolls according to the manufacturer's instructions. When hot, slice horizontally, three-quarters of the way through, and spread with the horseradish mixture. Fill the rolls with rocket and a sausage, then onion.

PREPARATION TIME: 15 MINUTES   COOKING TIME: 25 MINUTES

NOTE: If you can't get chipolatas, you can use thin sausages and twist them through the centre.

HERBED SCALLOP KEBABS

24 cleaned scallops (without roe)
6 large spring onions (scallions), green part only
2 zucchini (courgettes)
2 carrots
20 g (³/₄ oz) butter, melted
2 teaspoons lemon juice
1 tablespoon dry white wine
2 teaspoons mixed dried herbs
¹/₂ teaspoon onion powder

MAKES 24

Soak 24 wooden skewers in cold water for 30 minutes. Wash the scallops, slice or pull off any vein, membrane or hard white muscle, then pat dry with paper towels. Cut the spring onions in half lengthways, then into 8 cm (3 inch) lengths. Line a baking tray with foil.

Using a vegetable peeler, slice the zucchini and carrots lengthways into thin ribbons. Plunge the vegetable strips into a bowl of boiling water, leave for 1 minute, then drain. Plunge into a bowl of iced water and leave until cold. Drain and pat dry with paper towels.

Roll each scallop in a strip of the spring onion, carrot and zucchini and secure with a wooden skewer.

Combine the butter, lemon juice and wine in a small bowl. Brush over the scallops. Sprinkle with the combined herbs and onion powder. Put under a hot grill (broiler) for 5–10 minutes, or until the scallops are tender and cooked through.

PREPARATION TIME: 1 HOUR +   COOKING TIME: 10 MINUTES

NOTE: Scallops can be prepared several hours ahead. Refrigerate, covered, until needed.

PROSCIUTTO-WRAPPED SCALLOPS

16 cleaned scallops (without roe)
4 thin prosciutto slices

SERVES 4

Soak 24 wooden skewers in cold water for 30 minutes. Rinse the scallops and pat dry.

Cut the prosciutto into quarters, each large enough to enclose a scallop. Wrap around the scallops and thread in pairs onto small wooden skewers. Grill under a preheated grill (broiler), or on a barbecue grill plate for 5 minutes, turning a couple of times during cooking.

PREPARATION TIME: 10 MINUTES   COOKING TIME: 5 MINUTES

Herbed scallop kebabs

MARINATED SEAFOOD

500 g (1 lb 2 oz) raw prawns (shrimp)

500 g (1 lb 2 oz) mussels, scrubbed, beards removed

125 ml (4 fl oz/$\frac{1}{2}$ cup) white wine vinegar

3 bay leaves

500 g (1 lb 2 oz) small squid tubes, sliced

500 g (1 lb 2 oz) cleaned scallops (without roe)

2 garlic cloves, crushed

125 ml (4 fl oz/$\frac{1}{2}$ cup) extra virgin olive oil

60 ml (2 fl oz/$\frac{1}{4}$ cup) lemon juice

1 tablespoon white wine vinegar

1 teaspoon dijon mustard

1 tablespoon chopped flat-leaf (Italian) parsley

SERVES 8

Peel the prawns, leaving the tails intact. Gently pull out the dark vein from each prawn back, starting from the head end.

Discard any mussels that are already open. Put the vinegar, bay leaves, 750 ml (26 fl oz/3 cups) water and $\frac{1}{2}$ teaspoon salt in a large saucepan and bring to the boil. Add the squid and scallops, then reduce the heat to low and simmer for 2–3 minutes, or until the seafood has turned white. Remove the squid and scallops with a slotted spoon and put in a bowl.

Repeat the process with the prawns, cooking until just pink, then removing with a slotted spoon. Return the liquid to the boil and add the mussels. Cover, reduce the heat and simmer for 3 minutes, or until all the shells are open. Stir occasionally and discard any unopened mussels. Cool, remove the meat and add to the bowl.

Whisk the garlic and oil together with the lemon juice, vinegar, mustard and parsley. Pour over the seafood and toss well. Refrigerate for 1–2 hours before serving.

PREPARATION TIME: 40 MINUTES +   COOKING TIME: 10 MINUTES

NOTE: Seafood should never be overcooked or it will become tough.

GARLIC LAMB SKEWERS

600 g (1 lb 5 oz) trimmed lamb steaks
1 garlic bulb
1 red chilli, chopped
2 garlic cloves, crushed
60 ml (2 fl oz/¼ cup) oil

MAKES 35

Cut the lamb steaks into 2 cm (³/₄ inch) cubes and halve each garlic clove lengthways.

Thread 2 pieces of lamb and 2 slices of garlic alternately onto 35 small metal skewers.

Mix together the chilli, crushed garlic cloves and oil. Heat a chargrill pan and lightly brush with oil. Cook the skewers for 2–5 minutes, brushing occasionally with the garlic and chilli marinade.

PREPARATION TIME: 15 MINUTES   COOKING TIME: 5 MINUTES

MALAYSIAN LAMB SATAYS

500 g (1 lb 2 oz) lamb fillets
1 onion, roughly chopped
2 garlic cloves, crushed
2 cm (³/₄ inch) piece lemon grass stem, white part only
2 slices fresh galangal
1 teaspoon chopped fresh ginger
1 teaspoon ground cumin
½ teaspoon ground fennel
1 tablespoon ground coriander
1 teaspoon ground turmeric
1 tablespoon soft brown sugar
1 tablespoon lemon juice

MAKES 8

Trim any fat or silver sinew from the lamb fillets. Slice the meat across the grain into very thin strips (if you have time, leave the meat in the freezer for 30 minutes as this will make it easier to thinly slice).

In a food processor, combine the onion, garlic, lemon grass, galangal, ginger, cumin, fennel, coriander, turmeric, sugar and lemon juice and process until a smooth paste is formed. Transfer the paste to a shallow non-metallic dish and add the lamb, stirring to coat well. Cover and refrigerate overnight.

Thread the meat onto eight metal skewers and cook under a preheated grill (broiler) for 3–4 minutes each side, or until cooked. Brush regularly with the remaining marinade while cooking.

PREPARATION TIME: 30 MINUTES +   COOKING TIME: 10 MINUTES

SPICY ROAST CHICKEN

1.6 kg (3 lb 8 oz) whole chicken
3 teaspoons chopped red chilli
3 garlic cloves
2 teaspoons peppercorns, crushed
2 teaspoons soft brown sugar
2 tablespoons soy sauce
2 teaspoons ground turmeric
1 tablespoon lime juice
30 g (1 oz) butter, chopped

SERVES 4–6

Preheat the oven to 180°C (350°F/Gas 4). Using a large cleaver, cut the chicken in half by cutting down the backbone and along the breastbone. To prevent the wings from burning, tuck them underneath. Put the chicken, skin side up, on a rack in a roasting tin and roast for 30 minutes.

Meanwhile, combine the chilli, garlic, peppercorns and sugar in a food processor or mortar and pestle and process briefly, or pound, until smooth. Add the soy sauce, turmeric and lime juice, and process in short bursts, or stir if using a mortar and pestle, until combined.

Brush the spice mixture over the chicken, dot it with the butter pieces and roast for a further 25–30 minutes, or until cooked through and rich red. Serve at room temperature.

PREPARATION TIME: 20 MINUTES   COOKING TIME: 1 HOUR

TERIYAKI STEAK KEBABS

750 g (1 lb 10 oz) lean rump steak
125 ml (4 fl oz/¹/₂ cup) soy sauce
125 ml (4 fl oz/¹/₂ cup) sherry or sake
1 garlic clove, crushed
1 teaspoon ground ginger
1 teaspoon sugar
lime wedges, to serve

MAKES 24

Cut the steak into thin strips, 15 cm (6 inches) long and thread the slices onto 24 wooden skewers.

Combine the soy sauce, sherry or sake, garlic and ground ginger and sugar.

Put the steak in a shallow non-metallic dish and marinate in the soy sauce mixture for at least 1 hour in the refrigerator, then drain.

Cook the skewers on a preheated barbecue flatplate for 3–4 minutes each side. Serve with lime wedges.

PREPARATION TIME: 10 MINUTES +   COOKING TIME: 10 MINUTES

CHICKEN AND LEMON GRASS SKEWERS

1 kg (2 lb 4 oz) boneless, skinless chicken thigh
6 lemon grass stems
12 spring onion (scallion) bulbs
60 ml (2 fl oz/¹/₄ cup) soy sauce
60 ml (2 fl oz/¹/₄ cup) mirin
2 tablespoons sugar
1 lemon grass stem, white part only, thinly sliced
1 red chilli, seeded and finely chopped

MAKES 24

Cut the chicken into 2 cm (³/₄ inch) cubes. Trim the leaves off the lemon grass stems. Cut the thicker ends of the stems into 10 cm (4 inch) lengths, then into quarters lengthways. Cut the spring onion bulbs into quarters. Make a small slit in the centre of each chicken cube and through the onion pieces, to make threading easier. Thread pieces of chicken and onion onto the lemon grass stems alternately, using 2 pieces of each for each stem.

Mix together the soy sauce, mirin and sugar. Heat a chargrill or frying pan and cook the skewers for 3–5 minutes. Brush with half the soy mixture as they cook, turning frequently. Add the lemon grass and chilli to the remaining soy mixture and serve with the skewers, for dipping.

PREPARATION TIME: 10 MINUTES   COOKING TIME: 5 MINUTES

Teriyaki steak kebabs

CHICKEN DRUMSTICKS WITH RANCH DRESSING

32 small chicken drumsticks
1 tablespoon garlic salt
1 tablespoon onion powder
oil, for deep-frying
250 ml (9 fl oz/1 cup) tomato sauce (ketchup)
80 ml (2½ fl oz/⅓ cup) worcestershire sauce
40 g (1½ oz) butter, melted
1 tablespoon sugar
Tabasco sauce, to taste

RANCH DRESSING
250 g (9 oz/1 cup) whole-egg mayonnaise
250 g (9 oz/1 cup) sour cream
80 ml (2½ fl oz/⅓ cup) lemon juice
20 g (¾ oz/⅓ cup) snipped chives

MAKES 32

Remove the skin from the chicken and use a cleaver or large knife to cut off the knuckle. Wash the chicken thoroughly and pat dry with paper towels. Combine 1 tablespoon cracked black pepper, and the garlic salt and onion powder and rub some into each piece of chicken.

Fill a deep heavy-based frying pan one-third full of oil and heat the oil to 180°C (350°F), or when a cube of bread dropped into the oil turns golden brown in 15 seconds. Cook the chicken in batches for 2 minutes each batch, remove with tongs or a slotted spoon and drain on paper towels.

Transfer the chicken to a large non-metallic bowl or shallow dish. Combine the sauces, butter, sugar and Tabasco, pour over the chicken and stir to coat. Refrigerate, covered, for several hours or overnight. Prepare and heat the barbecue 1 hour before cooking.

Put the chicken on a lightly oiled hot barbecue grill or flatplate and cook for 20–25 minutes, or until cooked through. Turn and brush with the marinade during cooking. Serve with the ranch dressing.

To make the ranch dressing, combine the mayonnaise, sour cream, juice, chives, and season to taste.

PREPARATION TIME: 25 MINUTES +   COOKING TIME: 35 MINUTES

ROSEMARY TUNA KEBABS

3 tomatoes
1 tablespoon olive oil
2-3 small red chillies, seeded and chopped
3-4 garlic cloves, crushed
1 red onion, finely chopped
60 ml (2 fl oz/¼ cup) dry white wine or water
600 g (1 lb 5 oz) tinned chickpeas, rinsed and drained
3 tablespoons chopped oregano
4 tablespoons chopped flat-leaf (Italian) parsley
lemon wedges, to serve

TUNA KEBABS
1 kg (2 lb 4 oz) tuna fillet, cut into 4 cm (1½ inch) cubes
8 rosemary stalks, about 20 cm (8 inches) long, with leaves
olive oil, for brushing

SERVES 4

Cut the tomatoes into halves or quarters and scoop out the seeds. Roughly chop the flesh.

Heat the oil in a large non-stick frying pan. Add the chilli, garlic and red onion and stir over medium heat for 5 minutes, or until softened. Add the chopped tomato and the white wine or water. Cook over low heat for 10 minutes, or until the mixture is soft and pulpy and most of the liquid has evaporated.

Stir in the chickpeas with the oregano and parsley. Season to taste.

Heat a grill (broiler) or barbecue plate. Thread the tuna onto the rosemary stalks, lightly brush with oil, then cook, turning, for 3 minutes. Do not overcook or the tuna will be dry and fall apart. Serve with the chickpeas and lemon wedges.

PREPARATION TIME: 20 MINUTES   COOKING TIME: 20 MINUTES

NOTE: Swordfish, striped marlin or salmon are also suitable for this recipe.

FISH AND CUMIN KEBABS

750 g (1 lb 10 oz) skinless firm white fish fillets, such as blue-eye, snapper or perch
2 tablespoons olive oil
1 garlic clove, crushed
3 tablespoons chopped coriander (cilantro) leaves
2 teaspoons ground cumin

SERVES 4

Cut the fish fillets into 3 cm (1¼ inch) cubes. Thread on oiled skewers and set aside.

To make the marinade, combine the oil, garlic, coriander, cumin and 1 teaspoon ground black pepper in a small bowl. Brush the marinade over the fish, cover with plastic wrap and refrigerate for several hours, or overnight, turning occasionally. Drain, reserving the marinade. Season just before cooking.

Put the skewers on a hot, lightly oiled barbecue flatplate. Cook for 5-6 minutes, or until tender, turning once and brushing with reserved marinade several times during cooking.

PREPARATION TIME: 10 MINUTES +   COOKING TIME: 10 MINUTES

Rosemary tuna kebabs

BARBECUED QUAIL

6 quails
250 ml (9 fl oz/1 cup) dry red wine
2 celery stalks, including tops, chopped
1 carrot, chopped
1 small onion, chopped
1 bay leaf, torn into small pieces
1 teaspoon ground allspice
1 teaspoon dried thyme
2 garlic cloves, crushed
2 tablespoons olive oil
2 tablespoons lemon juice
lemon wedges, to serve

MAKES 24 PIECES

To prepare the quails, use poultry shears to cut down either side of the backbone, then discard the backbone. Remove the innards and neck, wash the insides and pat dry with paper towels. Place, breast side up, on the bench, open out flat and gently press to flatten. Using poultry shears, cut in half through the breast then cut each half in half again into the thigh and drumstick piece and breast and wing piece.

In a non-metallic bowl, combine the wine, celery, carrot, onion, bay leaf and allspice. Add the quail and stir to coat. Cover and refrigerate for 3 hours, or preferably overnight, stirring occasionally. Drain and sprinkle with thyme and salt and pepper.

Whisk together the garlic, oil and lemon juice in a small bowl.

Heat a lightly oiled barbecue plate until hot. Reduce the heat to medium and cook the quail breast pieces for 4–5 minutes each side and the drumstick pieces for 3 minutes each side, or until tender and cooked through. Brush frequently with the lemon mixture. Serve hot with lemon wedges.

PREPARATION TIME: 40 MINUTES +   COOKING TIME: 10 MINUTES

CHILLI PRAWN SKEWERS

30 large raw prawns (shrimp)
60 g (2¼ oz) butter
1 garlic clove, crushed
2 teaspoons soft brown sugar
2 tablespoons lemon or lime juice
2 tablespoons finely chopped coriander
(cilantro) sprigs
2 tablespoons finely chopped basil leaves
1 tablespoon sweet chilli sauce

MAKES 30

Peel the prawns, leaving the tails intact. Gently pull out the dark vein from each prawn back, starting from the head end.

Heat the butter in a large frying pan or wok. Add the garlic, sugar, juice, coriander, basil and sweet chilli sauce. Mix thoroughly, add the prawns in batches, then cook over medium heat for 5 minutes, or until the prawns turn pink and are cooked through.

Thread each prawn onto a bamboo skewer or strong toothpick to serve.

PREPARATION TIME: 25 MINUTES   COOKING TIME: 10 MINUTES

NOTES: Prepare the prawns several hours ahead. Cook just before serving.
   Scallops or oysters can be used instead of prawns, or alternate pieces of fish with prawns.

TANDOORI PRAWNS

1 kg (2 lb 4 oz) raw king prawns (about 24)
125 g (4½ oz/½ cup) plain yoghurt
20 g (¾ oz) finely chopped coriander
(cilantro) leaves
2 tablespoons finely chopped mint
1 tablespoon chopped fresh ginger
2 garlic cloves, crushed
1 teaspoon chilli powder
1 teaspoon ground turmeric
1 teaspoon ground coriander
1 teaspoon garam masala
few drops red food colouring (optional)
2 lemons, cut into wedges, to serve

MAKES 24

Peel the prawns, leaving the tails intact. Gently pull out the dark vein from each prawn back, starting from the head end. Rinse and pat dry with paper towels.

Combine the yoghurt with the fresh coriander, mint and salt, to taste. Pour over the prawns, mix well and leave for 5 minutes.

Mix the ginger, garlic, chilli powder, turmeric, coriander, garam masala and food colouring in a large bowl. Add the prawns and marinate for 10 minutes.

Thread one prawn onto a metal skewers and barbecue for about 5 minutes. Turn the skewers once, so the prawns cook evenly. They are ready when they start to curl and turn opaque. Serve on the skewers or loose with lemon wedges.

PREPARATION TIME: 20 MINUTES +   COOKING TIME: 5 MINUTES

Chilli prawn skewers

TANDOORI FISH CUTLETS

4 firm white fish cutlets, such as
blue-eye, snapper or perch
60 ml (2 fl oz/¼ cup) lemon juice
1 onion, finely chopped
2 garlic cloves, crushed
1 tablespoon grated fresh ginger
1 red chilli
1 tablespoon garam masala
1 teaspoon paprika
500 g (1 lb 2 oz/2 cups) Greek-style
yoghurt, plus extra to serve
few drops red food colouring (optional)
baby English spinach leaves, to serve
lime wedges, to serve

Pat the fish cutlets dry with paper towels and arrange in a shallow non-metallic dish. Drizzle the lemon juice over the fish and turn to coat the cutlets with the juice.

Blend the onion, garlic, ginger, chilli, garam masala, paprika and salt in a blender until smooth. Transfer to a bowl and stir in the yoghurt and the food colouring if using. Spoon the marinade over the fish and turn the fish to coat thoroughly. Cover and refrigerate overnight.

Heat a barbecue hotplate. Remove the cutlets from the marinade and allow any excess to drip off. Cook the cutlets on the barbecue, or under a grill (broiler), for 3–4 minutes each side, or until the fish flakes easily when tested with a fork. Serve with extra yoghurt, baby English spinach leaves and lime wedges.

SERVES 4   PREPARATION TIME: 15 MINUTES +   COOKING TIME: 10 MINUTES

FRIED CRISPY CHICKEN

4 chicken leg quarters or
8 drumsticks
4 garlic cloves, chopped
3 coriander (cilantro) roots, finely
chopped
2 teaspoons ground turmeric
1 teaspoon caster (superfine) sugar
2 tablespoons chilli sauce, plus extra
to serve (optional)
oil, for deep-frying

SERVES 4

Remove the skin from the chicken pieces. Put the chicken in a large saucepan with enough water to cover it. Cover and simmer for 15 minutes, or until cooked through. Drain and cool.

Put the garlic, coriander root, turmeric, 1 teaspoon pepper, 1 teaspoon salt, sugar and chilli sauce in a mortar and pestle or food processor and pound or process into a smooth paste. Brush over the chicken, cover and refrigerate for 30 minutes.

Heat the oil in a heavy-based frying pan, add the chicken in batches and cook until dark brown, turning frequently. Drain on paper towels. Serve hot or cold with chilli sauce, if desired.

PREPARATION TIME: 20 MINUTES +   COOKING TIME: 30 MINUTES

TAMARIND CHICKEN

4 boneless, skinless chicken thighs
4 chicken drumsticks
80 ml (2½ fl oz/⅓ cup) tamarind
concentrate
2 teaspoons ground coriander
1 teaspoon ground turmeric
2 garlic cloves, crushed
2 tablespoons peanut oil
2 red chillies, finely chopped
6 spring onions (scallions), finely chopped
oil, for deep-frying

SERVES 4

Remove the skin from the chicken pieces. Put the chicken in a large saucepan with enough water to cover it. Cover and simmer for 15 minutes, or until cooked through. Drain and cool.

Combine the tamarind, coriander, turmeric and garlic. Add the tamarind mixture to the chicken and toss well to coat. Cover and marinate in the refrigerator for at least 2 hours, or preferably overnight.

Heat the peanut oil in a frying pan; add the chilli and spring onion, and stir-fry over low heat for 3 minutes. Set aside.

Heat the oil in a large deep frying pan. Cook the chicken in three batches over medium heat for 5 minutes, or until the chicken is golden brown and heated through. Drain the chicken on paper towels, and keep warm while frying the remaining chicken. Serve the chicken pieces with a spoonful of the chilli mixture on the side.

PREPARATION TIME: 15 MINUTES +   COOKING TIME: 35 MINUTES

Fried crispy chicken

BARBECUED ASIAN-STYLE PRAWNS

500 g (1 lb 2 oz) large raw prawns
(shrimp)
lime wedges, to serve

MARINADE
2 tablespoons lemon juice
2 tablespoons sesame oil
2 garlic cloves, crushed
2 teaspoons grated fresh ginger

SERVES 4

Peel the prawns, leaving the tails intact. Gently pull out the dark vein from each prawn back, starting from the head end.

Mix the lemon juice, sesame oil, garlic and ginger in a bowl. Add the prawns and gently stir to coat the prawns. Cover and refrigerate for at least 3 hours.

Cook the prawns on a hot, lightly oiled barbecue plate for 3-5 minutes, or until pink and cooked through. Brush frequently with marinade while cooking. Serve immediately with the lime wedges.

PREPARATION TIME: 10 MINUTES +   COOKING TIME: 5 MINUTES

NOTES: Alternatively, the prawns can be threaded onto bamboo skewers. Soak the skewers in cold water for about 30 minutes, or until they sink. This will prevent the skewers burning during cooking. After marinating, thread the prawns evenly onto the skewers and cook as stated, turning and basting occasionally during cooking.

The amount of garlic can be altered, according to taste. For a stronger flavour, double the quantity of garlic and omit the ginger. For a spicy dish, substitute two finely chopped fresh chillies for the garlic.

You can also halve the quantity of prawns and add scallops.

SWEET TREATS AND DRINKS

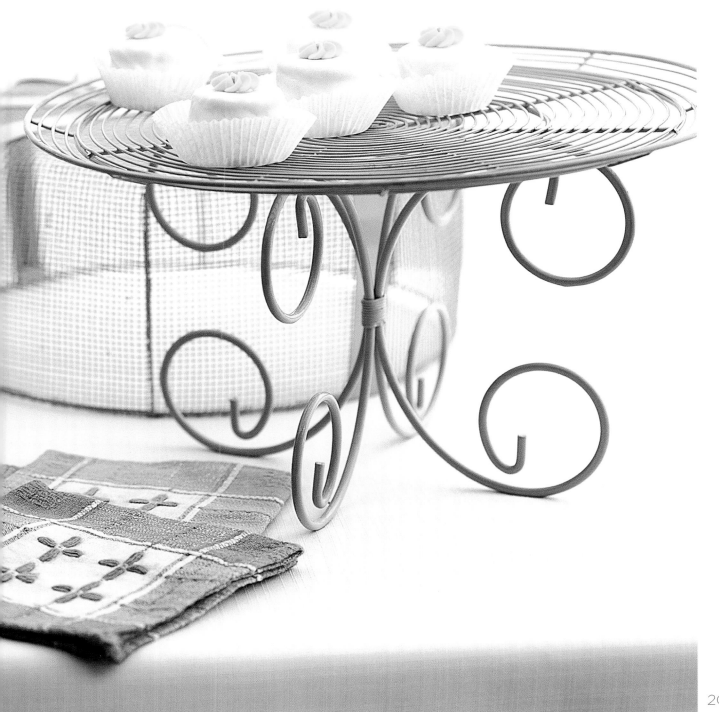

TURKISH DELIGHT

880 g (1 lb 15 oz/4 cups) sugar
125 g (4^1/$_2$ oz/1 cup) cornflour (cornstarch)
1 teaspoon cream of tartar
2 tablespoons rosewater
red food colouring
40 g (1^1/$_2$ oz/^{1}/$_3$ cup) icing (confectioners')
sugar

MAKES 25 PIECES

Pour 625 ml (21^1/$_2$ fl oz/2^1/$_2$ cups) water into a large heavy-based saucepan and bring to the boil. Add the sugar and stir until thoroughly dissolved. Remove from the heat.

In a large bowl, blend the cornflour and cream of tartar with 250 ml (9 fl oz/1 cup) cold water. Gradually add the blended cornflour to the sugar syrup, then return the saucepan to medium heat and stir until the mixture boils.

Reduce the heat and cook very slowly for 45 minutes, stirring often. During this time, the colour will change from cloudy to clear and golden, and the mixture will thicken.

Add the rosewater and a few drops of food colouring. Pour onto a lightly oiled 20 x 30 cm (8 x 12 inch) baking tray and leave to set. When firm and cool, cut into 2 cm (^{3}/$_4$ inch) squares and toss in the icing sugar.

PREPARATION TIME: 10 MINUTES   COOKING TIME: 1 HOUR

DATE CANDIES

150 g (5^1/$_2$ oz/1^1/$_2$ cups) walnut halves
2 tablespoons sesame seeds
100 g (3^1/$_2$ oz) ghee
600 g (1 lb 5 oz) pitted dried dates,
coarsely chopped

SERVES 6–8

Preheat the oven to 180°C (350°F/Gas 4) and line the base and two opposite sides of an 18 cm (7 inch) square slice tin with baking paper. Spread the walnuts on a baking tray and bake for 5 minutes, or until lightly toasted. Chop coarsely. Bake the sesame seeds until golden.

Melt the ghee in a large heavy-based saucepan and cook the dates, covered, over low heat for about 10 minutes, stirring often, until the dates soften. Using the back of a spoon dipped in cold water, spread half in the tin. Scatter the walnuts on top and press into the dates. Spread the remaining date mixture over the walnuts. Smooth the surface with wet fingers and press down firmly. Sprinkle with the sesame seeds and press lightly into the dates. When cool, cut into small diamonds.

PREPARATION TIME: 10 MINUTES +   COOKING TIME: 20 MINUTES

NOUGAT

440 g (15½ oz/2 cups) sugar
250 ml (9 fl oz/1 cup) liquid glucose
175 g (6 oz/½ cup) honey
2 egg whites
1 teaspoon natural vanilla extract
125 g (4½ oz) unsalted butter, softened
60 g (2¼ oz) almonds, unblanched and toasted
100 g (3½ oz) glacé cherries

MAKES 1 KG (2 LB 4 OZ)

Grease a 18 x 28 cm (7 x 11 inch) baking dish and line with baking paper. Put the sugar, glucose, honey, 60 ml (2 fl oz/¼ cup) water and ¼ teaspoon salt in a heavy-based saucepan and stir over low heat until dissolved. Bring to the boil and cook at a rolling boil for 8 minutes, or until the mixture reaches 122°C (225°F) on a sugar thermometer. The correct temperature is very important, otherwise the mixture will not set properly.

Beat the egg whites in a bowl with electric beaters until stiff peaks form. Slowly pour one-quarter of the sugar mixture onto the egg whites in a thin stream and beat for up to 5 minutes, or until the mixture holds its shape. Put the remaining syrup over the heat and cook for 2 minutes (watch that it doesn't burn), or until a small amount forms brittle threads when dropped in cold water, or reaches 157°C (315°F) on a sugar thermometer. Pour slowly onto the meringue mixture with the beaters running and beat until the mixture is very thick.

Add the vanilla and butter and beat for a further 5 minutes. Stir in the almonds and cherries with a metal spoon. Turn the mixture into the tin and smooth the top with a palate knife. Refrigerate for at least 4 hours, or until firm. Turn out onto a large chopping board and cut into 2 x 4 cm (¾ x 1½ inch) pieces. Wrap each piece in cellophane and store in the refrigerator.

PREPARATION TIME: 30 MINUTES +   COOKING TIME: 15 MINUTES

CHOCOLATE STRAWBERRIES

250 g (9 oz) strawberries
150 g (5¹/₂ oz) dark chocolate
100 g (3¹/₂ oz) white chocolate

SERVES 8–10

Brush the strawberries with a dry pastry brush to remove any dirt. Melt the dark chocolate in a small heatproof bowl over a saucepan of steaming water, making sure the base of the bowl does not touch the water. Dip the bottom half of each strawberry in the chocolate. Put on a baking tray lined with baking paper and allow to set.

When set, melt the white chocolate in the same way as the dark. Dip the tips of the strawberries in the chocolate and allow to set on the baking tray.

PREPARATION TIME: 10 MINUTES +   COOKING TIME: 5 MINUTES

WALNUT CHOCOLATES

100 g (3¹/₂ oz) walnut pieces
60 g (2¹/₄ oz/¹/₂ cup) icing (confectioners')
sugar
2 teaspoons egg white
200 g (7 oz) dark chocolate
30 walnut halves

MAKES 30

Chop the walnut pieces in a food processor. Sift the icing sugar and process with the walnuts and egg white until a moist paste forms. Cover and refrigerate for 20 minutes.

Roll teaspoons of the walnut paste into 30 balls and flatten slightly. Put the chocolate in a heatproof bowl. Bring a saucepan of water to the boil and remove from the heat. Sit the bowl over the pan, making sure the base of the bowl does not sit in the water. Stir occasionally until the chocolate has melted.

Dip the walnut rounds in the chocolate and transfer to a piece of baking paper or foil. Press the walnut halves gently into the top of each round and leave to set.

PREPARATION TIME: 30 MINUTES +   COOKING TIME: 5 MINUTES

NOTE: These chocolates will keep for up to 4 days.

Chocolate strawberries

CHOCOLATE CARROT SLICE

125 g (4$\frac{1}{2}$ oz/1 cup) self-raising flour
1 teaspoon ground cinnamon
170 g (6 oz/$\frac{3}{4}$ cup) caster (superfine)
sugar
80 g (2$\frac{3}{4}$ oz/$\frac{1}{2}$ cup) finely grated carrot
185 g (6$\frac{1}{2}$ oz/1 cup) mixed dried fruit
90 g (3$\frac{1}{4}$ oz/$\frac{1}{2}$ cup) chocolate chips
30 g (1 oz/$\frac{1}{3}$ cup) desiccated coconut
2 eggs, beaten
90 g (3$\frac{1}{4}$ oz) unsalted butter, melted
40 g (1$\frac{1}{2}$ oz/$\frac{1}{3}$ cup) chopped walnuts

CREAM CHEESE FROSTING
125 g (4$\frac{1}{2}$ oz) cream cheese
30 g (1 oz) unsalted butter
185 g (6$\frac{1}{2}$ oz/1$\frac{1}{2}$ cups) icing
(confectioners') sugar, sifted

MAKES 32

Preheat the oven to 180°C (350°F/Gas 4). Lightly grease a shallow 23 cm (9 inch) square cake tin and line the base and sides with baking paper.

Sift the flour and cinnamon into a large bowl. Add the caster sugar, grated carrot, mixed fruit, chocolate chips and coconut and stir until just combined. Add the beaten eggs and butter and then stir until combined.

Spread the mixture evenly into the prepared tin and smooth the surface. Bake for 30 minutes, or until golden. Allow to cool in the tin, then turn out onto a flat surface.

To make the cream cheese frosting, using electric beaters, beat the cream cheese and butter in a small bowl until smooth. Add the icing sugar and beat for 2 minutes, or until the mixture is light and fluffy. Add 1 teaspoon water and beat until well combined.

Spread the slice with frosting using a flat-bladed knife and sprinkle with walnuts. Cut into 16 squares, then cut each square into two triangles.

PREPARATION TIME: 20 MINUTES   COOKING TIME: 30 MINUTES

NOTES: This slice can be frozen for up to 2 months.
The topping may be sprinkled with grated chocolate, if desired.

MINI TOFFEE APPLES

2 large apples
200 g (7 oz) sugar

MAKES 6–8

Peel the apples and use a melon baller to cut out balls, or cut the apples into cubes. Push a cocktail stick into each ball or cube.

Sprinkle the sugar in an even layer over the base of a saucepan and melt over low heat, slowly tipping the pan from side to side to make sure the sugar melts evenly. Keep the sugar moving so it does not start to colour on one side before the other side has melted. When the caramel starts to colour, keep swirling until you have an even colour, then remove the pan from the heat and stop the cooking by plunging the base into cold water. Reheat the caramel gently until runny.

Dip each piece of apple in the caramel, coating completely. Leave to dry, standing upright on a piece of baking paper. Reheat the caramel when necessary.

PREPARATION TIME: 10 MINUTES   COOKING TIME: 10 MINUTES

JAM DROPS

80 g (2³/4 oz) unsalted butter, softened
80 g (2³/4 oz/¹/3 cup) caster (superfine) sugar
2 tablespoons milk
¹/2 teaspoon natural vanilla extract
125 g (4¹/2 oz/1 cup) self-raising flour
40 g (1¹/2 oz/¹/3 cup) custard powder
100 g (3¹/2 oz/¹/3 cup) raspberry jam

MAKES 32

Preheat the oven to 180°C (350°F/Gas 4). Line two baking trays with baking paper.

Cream the butter and sugar in a small bowl using electric beaters until light and fluffy. Add the milk and vanilla and beat until combined. Sift in the flour and custard powder and mix to form a soft dough. Roll heaped teaspoons of the mixture into balls and place on the trays.

Make an indentation in each ball using the end of a wooden spoon. Fill each hole with a little jam. Bake for 15 minutes, cool slightly on the trays, then transfer to a wire rack to cool.

PREPARATION TIME: 20 MINUTES   COOKING TIME: 15 MINUTES

APPLE CUSTARD STREUSEL SLICE

155 g (5½ oz/1¼ cups) plain (all-purpose) flour

1 tablespoon caster (superfine) sugar

80 g (2¾ oz) unsalted butter, melted and cooled

1 egg yolk

APPLE CUSTARD TOPPING

3 green apples

20 g (¾ oz) unsalted butter

80 g (2¾ oz/⅓ cup) caster (superfine) sugar

2 eggs

185 ml (6 fl oz/¾ cup) pouring (whipping) cream

1 teaspoon natural vanilla extract

CRUMBLE TOPPING

60 g (2¼ oz/½ cup) plain (all-purpose) flour

2 tablespoons dark brown sugar

40 g (1½ oz/⅓ cup) finely chopped walnuts

60 g (2¼ oz) unsalted butter, cubed

MAKES 16 PIECES

Lightly grease an 18 x 28 cm (7 x 11 inch) shallow tin and line with baking paper, leaving the paper hanging over the two long sides.

Sift the flour and sugar into a bowl. Add the butter, egg yolk and 2–3 tablespoons water and mix to form a ball. Roll out the dough between two sheets of baking paper and fit in the base of the tin. Refrigerate for 20 minutes. Preheat the oven to 190°C (375°F/Gas 5).

Line the pastry with baking paper, fill with baking beads or uncooked rice and bake for 15 minutes. Remove the paper and rice, reduce the oven to 180°C (350°F/Gas 4) and bake the pastry for 5 minutes, or until golden. Allow to cool.

Peel, core and chop the apples and put in a saucepan with the butter, half the sugar and 2 tablespoons water. Cover and cook over low heat for 15 minutes, or until soft. Uncover and simmer for a further 5 minutes to reduce the liquid. Use a wooden spoon to break down the apples until they have a smooth texture. Allow to cool.

Whisk together the eggs, cream, remaining sugar and natural vanilla extract. Spread the cooled apple over the pastry, then carefully pour on the cream mixture. Bake for 20 minutes, or until the custard has half set.

To make the crumble, mix the flour, sugar and walnuts and rub in the butter until the mixture is crumbly. Sprinkle over the custard and bake for 15 minutes. Cool in the tin before slicing into 16 pieces. These will keep in the fridge for up to 1 week.

PREPARATION TIME: 30 MINUTES +   COOKING TIME: 1 HOUR 15 MINUTES

BERRY ALMOND SLICE

1 sheet frozen puff pastry, thawed
150 g (5^1/$_2$ oz) unsalted butter
170 g (6 oz/^{3}/$_4$ cup) caster (superfine) sugar
3 eggs, beaten
2 tablespoons grated lemon zest
125 g (4^1/$_2$ oz/^{2}/$_3$ cup) ground almonds
2 tablespoons plain (all-purpose) flour
150 g (5^1/$_2$ oz) raspberries
150 g (5^1/$_2$ oz) blackberries
icing (confectioners') sugar, for dusting

MAKES 15 PIECES

Preheat the oven to 200°C (400°F/Gas 6). Lightly grease a 23 cm (9 inch) square shallow tin and line with baking paper, leaving the paper hanging over the two opposite sides.

Put the pastry on a baking tray lined with baking paper. Prick the pastry all over with a fork and bake for 15 minutes, or until golden. Ease into the tin, trimming the edges if necessary. Reduce the oven to 180°C (350°F/Gas 4).

Cream the butter and sugar in a small bowl using electric beaters until light and fluffy. Gradually add the egg, beating after every addition, then the lemon zest. Fold in the almonds and flour, then spread the mixture over the pastry.

Scatter the fruit on top and bake for 1 hour, or until lightly golden. Cool in the tin, then lift out, using the paper as handles. Cut into pieces and dust with icing sugar to serve.

PREPARATION TIME: 25 MINUTES   COOKING TIME: 1 HOUR 15 MINUTES

TOLLHOUSE COOKIES

180 g (6^1/$_2$ oz) unsalted butter, softened
140 g (5 oz/^{3}/$_4$ cup) soft brown sugar
110 g (3^3/$_4$ oz/^{1}/$_2$ cup) sugar
2 eggs, beaten
1 teaspoon natural vanilla extract
310 g (11 oz/2^1/$_4$ cups) plain (all-purpose) flour
1 teaspoon bicarbonate of soda (baking soda)
350 g (12 oz/2 cups) dark chocolate chips
100 g (3^1/$_2$ oz/1 cup) pecans, roughly chopped

MAKES 40

Preheat the oven to 190°C (375°F/Gas 5). Line two baking trays with baking paper.

Cream the butter and sugars in a large bowl using electric beaters until light and fluffy. Gradually add the egg, beating well after each addition. Stir in the vanilla, then the sifted flour and bicarbonate of soda until just combined. Mix in the chocolate chips and pecans.

Drop tablespoons of mixture onto the trays, leaving room for spreading. Bake the cookies for 8–10 minutes, or until lightly golden. Cool slightly on the trays before transferring to a wire rack to cool completely. When completely cold, store in an airtight container.

PREPARATION TIME: 20 MINUTES   COOKING TIME: 20 MINUTES

NOTE: You can use any nuts such as walnuts, almonds or hazelnuts.

Berry almond slice

FAMILY-STYLE GINGERBREAD PEOPLE

125 g (4¹/₂ oz) unsalted butter, softened
60 g (2¹/₄ oz/¹/₃ cup) soft brown sugar
90 g (3¹/₄ oz/¹/₄ cup) golden syrup or maple syrup
1 egg, lightly beaten
250 g (9 oz/2 cups) plain (all-purpose) flour
30 g (1 oz/¹/₄ cup) self-raising flour
1 tablespoon ground ginger
1 teaspoon bicarbonate of soda (baking soda)
1 tablespoon currants

ICING
1 egg white
¹/₂ teaspoon lemon juice
155 g (5¹/₂ oz/1¹/₄ cups) icing (confectioners') sugar, sifted
assorted food colourings

MAKES 16

Preheat the oven to 180°C (350°F/Gas 4). Line two baking trays with baking paper.

Cream the butter, sugar and golden syrup in a small bowl using electric beaters until light and fluffy. Add the egg gradually, beating well after each addition. Transfer to a large bowl. Sift the dry ingredients onto the butter mixture and mix with a knife until just combined. Combine the dough with well-floured hands. Turn onto a well-floured surface and knead for 1–2 minutes, or until smooth. Roll out the dough on a chopping board, between two sheets of baking paper, to 5 mm (¹/₄ inch) thick. Refrigerate on the board for 15 minutes to firm.

Cut the dough into shapes with a 13 cm (5 inch) gingerbread person cutter. Press the remaining dough together and re-roll. Cut out shapes and put the biscuits on the trays. Put currants as eyes and noses. Bake for 10 minutes, or until lightly browned. Cool completely on the trays.

To make the icing, beat the egg white using electric beaters in a small, clean, dry bowl until foamy. Gradually add the lemon juice and icing sugar and beat until thick and creamy. Divide the icing among several bowls. Tint the mixture with food colourings and spoon into small paper piping (icing) bags. Seal the open ends, snip the tips off the bags and pipe on faces and clothing.

PREPARATION TIME: 40 MINUTES +   COOKING TIME: 10 MINUTES

NOTE: When the icing is completely dry, store the biscuits in an airtight container in a cool, dry place for up to 3 days.

LITTLE LEMON TARTS

250 g (9 oz/2 cups) plain (all-purpose) flour
125 g (4¹/₂ oz) unsalted butter, chopped
2 teaspoons caster (superfine) sugar
1 teaspoon grated lemon zest
1 egg yolk

FILLING
125 g (4¹/₂ oz) cream cheese, softened
115 g (4 oz/¹/₂ cup) caster (superfine) sugar
2 egg yolks
2 tablespoons lemon juice
160 g (5³/₄ oz/¹/₂ cup) sweetened condensed milk
strips of candied lemon peel, to garnish

MAKES 24

Preheat the oven to 180°C (350°F/Gas 4). Brush two round-based 12-cup shallow patty pans or mini muffin tins with oil. Sift the flour and a pinch of salt into a bowl and rub in the butter. Add the sugar, zest, egg yolk and 2–3 tablespoons iced water and mix with a knife. Gently knead on a lightly floured surface until smooth. Cover in plastic wrap and chill for 10 minutes.

To make the filling, beat the combined cream cheese, sugar and egg yolks using electric beaters until smooth and thickened. Add the lemon juice and condensed milk and beat until well combined.

Roll out the dough between sheets of baking paper to 3 mm (about ¹/₈ inch) thickness. Using a 7 cm (2³/₄ inch) fluted round cutter, cut rounds from the pastry. Gently press into the patty tins. Lightly prick each round three times with a fork. Bake for 10 minutes, or until just starting to turn golden. Remove from the oven and spoon 2 teaspoons of filling into each case. Return to the oven for a further 5 minutes, or until the filling has set. Cool slightly before removing from the tins. Garnish with strips of candied lemon peel, if desired.

PREPARATION TIME: 40 MINUTES +   COOKING TIME: 15 MINUTES

FAST CHOCOLATE FUDGE COOKIES

90 g (3¹/₄ oz/³/₄ cup) plain (all-purpose) flour
60 g (2¹/₄ oz/¹/₂ cup) self-raising flour
125 g (4¹/₂ oz/1 cup) chopped walnuts
90 g (3¹/₄ oz/¹/₂ cup) chocolate chips
125 g (4¹/₂ oz) unsalted butter, melted
200 g (7 oz) dark chocolate, melted
2 tablespoons golden syrup or honey
2 eggs, beaten

MAKES ABOUT 30

Preheat the oven to 180°C (350°F/Gas 4). Sift the flours into a large bowl. Stir in the walnuts and chocolate chips.

Make a well in the centre of the dry ingredients. Add the butter, dark chocolate, golden syrup and eggs. Stir until combined.

Drop level tablespoonsfuls onto a lightly greased baking tray. Leave about 4 cm (1¹/₂ inches) between each cookie to allow for spreading. Bake for 12 minutes, then transfer to a wire rack to cool.

PREPARATION TIME: 20 MINUTES   COOKING TIME: 15 MINUTES

PETITS FOURS

2 eggs
55 g (2 oz/¹/₄ cup) caster (superfine) sugar
85 g (3 oz/²/₃ cup) plain (all-purpose) flour
30 g (1 oz) unsalted butter, melted

TOPPING
315 g (11 oz/1 cup) apricot jam, warmed and strained
2 teaspoons liqueur
200 g (7 oz) marzipan
400 g (14 oz) ready-made soft icing, chopped
small coloured fondant flowers, to decorate (optional)

MAKES 32

Preheat the oven to 180°C (350°F/Gas 4). Lightly grease two 4.5 x 8 x 26 cm (1³/₄ x 3 x 10¹/₂ inch) loaf (bar) tins. Line the bases and sides with baking paper.

Beat the eggs and sugar in a bowl using electric beaters for 5 minutes, until very thick and pale. Fold in the sifted flour and melted butter quickly and lightly, using a metal spoon. Divide between the tins and bake for 15 minutes, or until lightly golden and springy to the touch. Leave in the tins for 3 minutes before turning out onto a wire rack to cool.

Using a 3 cm (1¹/₄ inch) round cutter, cut shapes from the cakes. Brush the top and sides of each with the combined jam and liqueur. Roll the marzipan out to a thickness of 2 mm (¹/₈ inch) and cut out rounds and strips to cover the top and sides of the cakes.

Put the icing and 2 tablespoons water in a heatproof bowl and stand the bowl over a saucepan of simmering water. Stir until the icing has melted and the mixture is smooth. Allow to cool slightly.

Put the marzipan-covered cakes on a wire rack over a tray. Spoon the icing over each cake and use a flat-bladed knife to spread evenly over the base and sides. Reheat the icing over the saucepan if it begins to thicken. Leave the cakes to set. Carefully lift from the rack and put each in a paper petit four case. Decorate with small coloured fondant flowers, if desired.

PREPARATION TIME: 45 MINUTES   COOKING TIME: 20 MINUTES

NOTES: Fondant flowers for decorating are found in some supermarkets and in speciality shops.

Petits fours will keep for up to 2 days in an airtight container in a cool, dark place. Store in a single layer.

COCONUT SEMOLINA SLICE

50 g (1³/₄ oz) sesame seeds
125 g (4¹/₂ oz/1 cup) fine semolina
230 g (8¹/₂ oz/1 cup) caster (superfine) sugar
750 ml (26 fl oz/3 cups) coconut cream
2 tablespoons ghee or oil
2 eggs, separated
¹/₄ teaspoon ground cardamom
fresh fruit, to serve (optional)

SERVES 8–10

Preheat the oven to 160°C (315°F/Gas 2–3). Lightly grease a 18 x 28 cm (7 x 11 inch) shallow tin.

Toast the sesame seeds in a dry frying pan over medium heat for 3–4 minutes, shaking the pan gently, until the seeds are golden brown; remove from the pan at once to prevent burning.

Put the semolina, sugar and coconut cream in a large saucepan and stir over medium heat for 5 minutes, or until boiling. Add the ghee or oil and continue stirring until the mixture comes away from the sides of the pan. Set aside to cool.

Beat the egg whites until stiff peaks form. Fold the egg whites, egg yolks and cardamom into the cooled semolina mixture. Spoon the mixture into the prepared tin and sprinkle with the sesame seeds. Bake for 45 minutes, or until golden brown. Cut into diamond shapes and serve with fresh fruit, if desired.

PREPARATION TIME: 20 MINUTES   COOKING TIME: 1 HOUR

MACADAMIA BLONDIES

100 g (3¹/₂ oz) unsalted butter, chopped
100 g (3¹/₂ oz) white chocolate, chopped
115 g (4 oz/¹/₂ cup) caster (superfine) sugar
2 eggs, beaten
1 teaspoon natural vanilla extract
125 g (4¹/₂ oz/1 cup) self-raising flour
80 g (2³/₄ oz/¹/₂ cup) macadamia nuts, roughly chopped
melted white chocolate, to serve (optional)

MAKES 25 PIECES

Preheat the oven to 180°C (350°F/Gas 4). Lightly grease a 20 cm (8 inch) square tin and line with baking paper, leaving the paper hanging over the two opposite sides.

Put the butter and white chocolate in a heatproof bowl. Half-fill a saucepan with water and bring to the boil. Remove from the heat. Put the bowl over the saucepan, making sure the base of the bowl does not touch the water. Stir occasionally until the butter and chocolate have melted and are smooth.

Add the caster sugar to the bowl and stir in the eggs. Add the vanilla, fold in the flour and macadamia nuts, then pour into the tin. Bake for 35–40 minutes. If the top starts to brown too quickly, cover with a sheet of foil. When cooked, cool in the tin before lifting out, using the paper as handles, and cutting into squares. Drizzle with melted white chocolate.

PREPARATION TIME: 20 MINUTES   COOKING TIME: 45 MINUTES

Coconut semolina slice

ALMOND FRIANDS

160 g (5³/4 oz) unsalted butter
90 g (3¹/4 oz/1 cup) flaked almonds
40 g (1¹/2 oz/¹/3 cup) plain (all-purpose) flour
165 g (5³/4 oz/1¹/3 cups) icing (confectioners') sugar
5 egg whites
icing (confectioners') sugar, for dusting

MAKES 10

Preheat the oven to 210°C (415°F/Gas 6–7). Lightly grease ten 125 ml (4 fl oz/¹/2 cup) friand tins.

Melt the butter in a small saucepan over medium heat. Cook for 3–4 minutes, or until the butter turns deep golden. Strain to remove any residue (the colour will deepen on standing). Remove from the heat and set aside to cool until just lukewarm.

Put the almonds in a food processor and process until finely ground. Transfer to a bowl and sift the flour and icing sugar into the same bowl.

Put the egg whites in a separate bowl and lightly whisk with a fork until just combined. Add the butter to the flour mixture along with the egg whites. Mix gently with a metal spoon until all the ingredients are well combined.

Spoon some mixture into each friand tin to fill to three-quarters. Put the tins on a baking tray and bake in the centre of the oven for 10 minutes, then reduce the heat to 180°C (350°F/Gas 4) and bake for a further 5 minutes, or until a skewer comes out clean when inserted in the centre of a friand. Remove and leave to cool in the tins for 5 minutes before turning out onto a wire rack to cool completely. Dust with icing sugar before serving.

PREPARATION TIME: 10 MINUTES   COOKING TIME: 20 MINUTES

NOTES: These friands will keep well for up to 3 days in an airtight container.

To make berry friands, make the mixture as above and put a fresh or frozen raspberry or blueberry on the top of each friand before placing in the oven.

To make lemon friands, add 2 teaspoons grated lemon zest to the flour and sugar mixture and proceed as above.

COCONUT MACAROONS

3 egg whites
310 g (11 oz) caster (superfine) sugar
1 teaspoon grated lemon zest
$^1/_2$ teaspoon coconut extract
2 tablespoons sifted cornflour
(cornstarch)
270 g (9$^3/_4$ oz/3 cups) desiccated coconut

MAKES 60

Preheat the oven to 160°C (315°F/Gas 2–3). Line two baking trays with baking paper.

Beat the egg whites in a dry bowl using electric beaters until soft peaks form. Gradually add the caster sugar, beating constantly until thick and glossy and the sugar has dissolved. Add the lemon zest and coconut extract and beat until just combined. Add the cornflour and desiccated coconut and stir gently with a metal spoon.

Drop heaped teaspoons onto the trays, about 3 cm (1$^1/_4$ inches) apart. Bake for 15–20 minutes, or until golden. Transfer to a wire rack to cool. Repeat with the remaining mixture.

PREPARATION TIME: 25 MINUTES   COOKING TIME: 40 MINUTES

CARAMEL SLICE

125 g (4$^1/_2$ oz/1 cup) self-raising flour
90 g (3$^1/_4$ oz/1 cup) desiccated coconut
115 g (4 oz/$^1/_2$ cup) caster (superfine) sugar
125 g (4$^1/_2$ oz) unsalted butter, melted

CARAMEL FILLING
400 g (14 oz) tinned sweetened condensed milk
20 g ($^3/_4$ oz) unsalted butter
2 tablespoons golden syrup or honey

CHOCOLATE TOPPING
150 g (5$^1/_2$ oz) dark chocolate, chopped
20 g ($^3/_4$ oz) Copha (white vegetable shortening)

MAKES 20 PIECES

Preheat the oven to 180°C (350°F/Gas 4). Lightly grease an 18 x 28 cm (7 x 11 inch) shallow tin and line with baking paper, leaving the paper hanging over on the two long sides.

Sift the flour into a bowl, then mix in the coconut and sugar. Add the melted butter to the bowl and stir through thoroughly. Press firmly into the tin and bake for 12–15 minutes, or until lightly coloured. Allow to cool.

To make the caramel filling, put all the ingredients in a saucepan over low heat. Slowly bring to the boil, stirring, then boil gently, stirring, for 4–5 minutes, or until lightly caramelized. Quickly pour over the cooled base, spreading evenly. Bake for 10 minutes, then set aside to cool in the tin.

To make the chocolate topping, put the dark chocolate and Copha in a heatproof bowl. Half-fill a saucepan with water and bring to the boil. Remove from the heat and sit the bowl over the saucepan, making sure the base of the bowl does not touch the water. Stir occasionally until melted. Spread over the caramel slice. Refrigerate for 20 minutes, or until set. Lift the slice from the tin and cut into pieces.

PREPARATION TIME: 30 MINUTES +   COOKING TIME: 35 MINUTES

MINI PAVLOVAS

3 egg whites
125 g (4½ oz/1 cup) icing (confectioners')
sugar
150 g (5½ oz) dark chocolate, melted
250 ml (9 fl oz/1 cup) thick
(double/heavy) cream
1 tablespoon icing (confectioners') sugar,
extra
1 teaspoon finely grated orange zest
assorted fresh fruit, to garnish, such as
strawberries, cut into thin wedges,
sliced pawpaw and kiwi fruit, and
passionfruit pulp

MAKES 35–40

Preheat the oven to 150°C (300°F/Gas 2). Beat the egg whites in a large bowl until stiff peaks form. Add the icing sugar to the egg whites while continuing to beat. Add it carefully or it will fly all over the place. At this stage it is best to use electric beaters as you must now beat the meringue until thick and very solid.

Using a cutter as a guide, draw about forty 4 cm (1½ inch) circles onto two sheets of baking paper, then invert these sheets onto baking trays (so the pencil won't come off on the base of the pavlovas). Spread a little of the meringue mixture over each round – this will be the base of the pavlova. Spoon the remaining meringue into a piping (icing) bag fitted with a 5 mm (¼ inch) plain piping nozzle.

Pipe three small circles on top of each other on the outer edge of each base, leaving a small hole in the centre. Bake for 30 minutes, or until firm to touch. Leave to cool in the oven with the door slightly ajar.

When cold, dip the bases of the meringues into the melted chocolate to come about 2 mm (⅛ inch) up the sides of the meringues, then place on trays covered with baking paper and allow to set.

Combine the cream, extra icing sugar and orange zest, stirring until just thick. If necessary, beat slightly. Spoon into a piping bag fitted with a small plain nozzle and pipe into the meringues. Top with fruit and passionfruit pulp.

PREPARATION TIME: 50 MINUTES +   COOKING TIME: 30 MINUTES

NOTE: Chocolate-dipped meringues without the filling can be made up to a week ahead and stored in an airtight container. Fill them close to serving time, otherwise they will soften.

FAST LEMON SHORTBREADS

125 g (4¹/2 oz/1 cup) plain (all-purpose) flour
1 tablespoon rice flour
100 g (3¹/2 oz) unsalted butter, chilled and chopped
¹/2 teaspoon finely grated lemon zest
1 tablespoon lemon juice

MAKES ABOUT 20

Preheat the oven to 180°C (350°F/Gas 4). Put the flours, butter and lemon zest into a food processor. Add the lemon juice and process until combined.

Roll out onto a lightly floured surface to a thickness of 5 mm (¹/4 inch). Cut out the desired shapes and place on a baking tray lined with baking paper. Bake for 10–12 minutes, or until pale golden. Allow to cool on a wire rack.

PREPARATION TIME: 10 MINUTES   COOKING TIME: 15 MINUTES

SWEET TWISTS

1 egg
1¹/2 tablespoons sugar
125 ml (4 fl oz/¹/2 cup) milk
250 g (9 oz/2 cups) plain (all-purpose) flour
oil, for deep-frying
215 g (7¹/2 oz/1³/4 cups) icing (confectioners') sugar

MAKES 45

Beat the egg with the sugar in a bowl, then stir in the milk. Sift the flour with ¹/2 teaspoon salt and mix in to form a stiff dough, adding more milk if necessary.

Roll out on a lightly floured work surface. Cut into strips about 10 cm (4 inches) long and 3 cm (1¹/4 inches) wide. Make a slit along the length, like a buttonhole. Tuck one end through the slit and pull through to make a twist.

Fill a deep heavy-based frying pan one-third full of oil and heat the oil to 180°C (350°F), or when a cube of bread dropped into the oil turns golden brown in 15 seconds. Fry three of four twists at a time, until golden brown on both sides. Drain on crumpled paper towels. Sift the icing sugar over the pastry after it is fried but before it gets cold.

PREPARATION TIME: 40 MINUTES   COOKING TIME: 10 MINUTES

NOTE: These will keep for up to 2 weeks in a dry airtight container.

Fast lemon shortbreads

NUTMEG DATE CAKE

370 g (13 oz/2 cups) soft brown sugar, plus 2 tablespoons extra
250 g (9 oz/2 cups) plain (all-purpose) flour
2 teaspoons baking powder
125 g (4¹/₂ oz) unsalted butter, chilled and chopped
1 teaspoon bicarbonate soda (baking soda)
185 ml (6 fl oz/³/₄ cup) milk
2 eggs, beaten
1¹/₂ teaspoons freshly grated nutmeg
375 g (12 oz) dried dates, roughly chopped
icing (confectioners') sugar, for dusting
whipped cream, to serve

SERVES 8–10

Preheat the oven to 180°C (350°F/Gas 4). Lightly grease a 22 cm (8¹/₂ inch) spring-form cake tin and line the base with baking paper.

Process the brown sugar with the flour and baking powder in a food processor for 10 seconds. Add the butter. Process for a further 10 seconds until the mixture resembles fine crumbs. Press half the mixture into the base of the prepared tin.

Dissolve the soda in the milk. Add the eggs and nutmeg and whisk. Pour the mixture into the remaining brown sugar and flour mixture and process for a further 10 seconds. Pour into the cake tin and scatter half the dates over the top. Bake for 55 minutes. Cool in the tin for 10 minutes. Remove from the tin and cool on a wire rack.

Put the remaining dates on top of the cake, sprinkle with the extra brown sugar and put under a very hot grill (broiler) for 1 minute, or until the sugar begins to melt. Allow to cool. Dust the top with icing sugar and serve with whipped cream.

PREPARATION TIME: 25 MINUTES   COOKING TIME: 1 HOUR

FLOURLESS CHOCOLATE FRUIT AND NUT CAKE

5 egg whites
170 g (6 oz/³/₄ cup) caster (superfine) sugar
100 g (3¹/₂ oz) glacé apricots, chopped
100 g (3¹/₂ oz) glacé figs, chopped
80 g (2³/₄ oz) glacé ginger, chopped
250 g (9 oz) blanched almonds, finely chopped
250 g (9 oz) dark chocolate, chopped
60 g (2¹/₄ oz) dark chocolate, melted
375 ml (12 fl oz/1¹/₂ cups) pouring (whipping) cream
chocolate leaves, to decorate (optional)

SERVES 8–10

Preheat oven to 150°C (300°F/Gas 2). Lightly grease a deep 24 cm (9¹/₂ inch) round spring-form cake tin and line the base and side with baking paper.

Beat the egg whites in a bowl using electric beaters until soft peaks form. Gradually add the sugar, beating well after each addition. Beat until the sugar has dissolved and the mixture is thick and glossy.

Using a metal spoon, fold in the fruits, ginger, almonds, and both the chopped and melted chocolate. Stir until just combined. Spread in the tin and bake for 1 hour, or until a skewer comes out clean when inserted in centre. Cool in the tin for 15 minutes. Remove from the tin and cool on a wire rack.

Whip the cream in a bowl using electric beaters until stiff peaks form. Using a piping (icing) bag with a plain nozzle, pipe swirls of cream on top of the cake. Decorate with chocolate leaves, if desired.

PREPARATION TIME: 40 MINUTES +   COOKING TIME: 1 HOUR

ALMOND TORTE

450 g (1 lb) blanched whole almonds, lightly toasted
150 g (5¹/₂ oz) unsalted butter, softened
400 g (14 oz) caster (superfine) sugar
6 eggs
150 g (5¹/₂ oz) plain (all-purpose) flour
2 teaspoons lemon zest
2 tablespoons lemon juice
icing (confectioners') sugar, for dusting

SERVES 8

Preheat the oven to 170°C (325°F/Gas 3). Lightly grease a 24 cm (9¹/₂ inch) spring-form cake tin. Grind the almonds finely in a food processor and set aside.

Cream the butter and sugar in a bowl using electric beaters until light and fluffy. Add the eggs one at a time, beating well after each addition. Using a large metal spoon, fold in the flour, ground almonds and the lemon zest. Stir until just combined and almost smooth.

Pour the batter into the prepared tin and bake for 1 hour 20 minutes, or until a skewer inserted in the centre comes out clean. Allow to cool for 5 minutes, then brush the top with lemon juice. Remove to a wire rack and allow to cool completely. Dust with icing sugar.

PREPARATION TIME: 15 MINUTES +   COOKING TIME: 1 HOUR 20 MINUTES

Flourless chocolate fruit and nut cake

RASPBERRY SWIRL CHEESECAKE

250 g (9 oz) plain sweet biscuits (cookies)
90 g (3¼ oz) unsalted butter, melted

FILLING
2 tablespoons powdered gelatine
500 g (1 lb 2 oz) light cream cheese, softened
80 ml (2½ fl oz/⅓ cup) lemon juice
115 g (4 oz/½ cup) caster (superfine) sugar
315 ml (10¾ fl oz/1¼ cups) whipped cream
250 g (9 oz) frozen raspberries
2 tablespoons caster (superfine) sugar, extra
whipped cream, to decorate (optional)
raspberries, to decorate (optional)

SERVES 8–10

Lightly grease a 23 cm (9 inch) spring-form cake tin and line the base with baking paper.

Finely crush the biscuits in a food processor, then mix in the butter. Spoon into the tin and press firmly over the base and up the side. Refrigerate for 20 minutes, or until firm.

To make the filling, put 60 ml (2 fl oz/¼ cup) water in a small heatproof bowl, sprinkle evenly with the gelatine and leave to go spongy. Bring a large saucepan filled with about 4 cm (1½ inches) water to the boil, remove from the heat, carefully lower the gelatine bowl into the water (it should come halfway up the side of the bowl), then stir until dissolved. Allow to cool.

Beat the cream cheese using electric beaters until creamy. Add the juice and sugar and beat until smooth. Gently fold in the whipped cream and half the gelatine.

Process the raspberries and extra sugar in a food processor until smooth. Push the purée through a fine-meshed nylon sieve to remove any pips. Fold the remaining gelatine into the raspberry mixture. Put blobs of cream cheese mixture into the tin and fill the gaps with the raspberry. Swirl the two mixtures together, using a skewer or the point of a knife. Refrigerate for 4 hours, or until set. Decorate with whipped cream and raspberries, if desired.

PREPARATION TIME: 40 MINUTES +   COOKING TIME: NIL

CHERRY CHEESE STRUDEL

500 g (1 lb 2 oz) ricotta cheese
2 teaspoons grated lemon or orange zest
55 g (2 oz/$\frac{1}{4}$ cup) sugar
40 g (1$\frac{1}{2}$ oz/$\frac{1}{2}$ cup) fresh white breadcrumbs
2 tablespoons ground almonds
2 eggs
425 g (15 oz) tinned pitted black cherries
2 teaspoons cornflour (cornstarch)
8 sheets filo pastry
60 g (2$\frac{1}{4}$ oz) unsalted butter, melted
2 tablespoons dry white breadcrumbs
icing (confectioners') sugar, for dusting

SERVES 8–10

Preheat the oven to 180°C (350°F/Gas 4). Lightly grease a baking tray.

Combine the ricotta, zest, sugar, fresh breadcrumbs and almonds in a bowl. Add the eggs and mix well. Drain the cherries, reserving half the juice. Blend the cornflour with the reserved cherry juice in a saucepan. Stir over medium heat until the mixture boils and thickens, then cool slightly.

Layer the pastry sheets, brushing between each sheet with melted butter and sprinkling with a few dry breadcrumbs. Form a large square by placing the second sheet halfway down the first sheet. Alternate layers, brushing with melted butter and sprinkling with breadcrumbs.

Put the ricotta mixture along one long edge of the pastry. Shape into a log and top with cherries and cooled syrup. Roll the pastry around the ricotta filling, folding in the edges as you roll. Finish with a pastry edge underneath. Place on the prepared tray and bake for 35–40 minutes, or until the pastry is golden. Dust with icing sugar. Serve cold, cut into slices.

PREPARATION TIME: 25 MINUTES   COOKING TIME: 45 MINUTES

WALNUT CAKES

200 g (7 oz) unsalted butter, softened
115 g (4 oz/$\frac{1}{2}$ cup) caster (superfine) sugar
2 tablespoons orange flower water
250 g (9 oz/2 cups) plain (all-purpose) flour, sifted

WALNUT FILLING
50 g (1$\frac{3}{4}$ oz/$\frac{1}{2}$ cup) walnuts, chopped
55 g (2 oz/$\frac{1}{4}$ cup) caster (superfine) sugar
1 teaspoon ground cinnamon

MAKES 28

Preheat the oven to 160°C (315°F/Gas 2–3). Lightly grease two baking trays and line with baking paper.

Cream the butter and sugar in a bowl using electric beaters until light and fluffy. Fold in the orange flower water and flour until combined. Press with your hands until the mixture comes together to make a stiff dough.

To make the walnut filling, combine all the ingredients in a bowl and mix well.

Roll heaped tablespoons of dough into balls. Press a hollow in the centre with your thumb. Place 1 teaspoon of filling into each hollow. Place on the trays and flatten slightly without folding dough over the filling. Bake for 15–20 minutes, or until golden. Cool on a wire rack and serve.

PREPARATION TIME: 15 MINUTES   COOKING TIME: 20 MINUTES

Cherry cheese strudel

RED FRUIT SALAD

250 g (9 oz) strawberries, halved
125 g (4$\frac{1}{2}$ oz) raspberries
250 g (9 oz) cherries, pitted
1 tablespoon Cointreau
1 tablespoon soft brown sugar

SERVES 4

Put the fruit in a bowl, drizzle with Cointreau, cover and set aside for 20 minutes.

Combine the sugar with 2 tablespoons water in a small saucepan over gentle heat for 3 minutes, or until dissolved. Cool, pour over the fruit and serve.

PREPARATION TIME: 10 MINUTES +   COOKING TIME: 5 MINUTES

EASTERN FRUIT PLATTER

1 lemon grass stem, white part only, chopped

2 cm (³/₄ inch) piece fresh ginger, roughly chopped

1 teaspoon soft brown sugar

125 ml (4 fl oz/¹/₂ cup) coconut milk

2 mangoes

1 nashi pear, quartered

6 lychees or rambutans, halved and stones removed

¹/₂ pawpaw, seeded and cut into wedges

¹/₂ red papaya, seeded and cut into wedges

2 star fruit, thickly sliced

1 lime, quartered

SERVES 4–6

Simmer the lemon grass, ginger, sugar and coconut milk in a small saucepan over low heat for 5 minutes. Strain and set aside.

Cut down both sides of the mangoes close to the stones. Score a crisscross pattern into each half, without cutting through the skin. Fold the outer edges under, pushing the centre up from underneath. Arrange with the rest of the fruit on a platter. Add the lime, for squeezing on the fruit.

Serve the coconut dressing on the side as a dipping sauce or drizzle over just before serving.

PREPARATION TIME: 15 MINUTES   COOKING TIME: 5 MINUTES

SUMMER FRUIT COMPOTE

5 apricots, halved

4 nectarines, halved

4 blood plums or other plums, stoned

4 peaches, quartered

200 g (7 oz) tinned pitted cherries

250 ml (9 fl oz/1 cup) claret

80 ml (2¹/₂ fl oz/¹/₃ cup) dry sherry

170 g (6 oz/³/₄ cup) caster (superfine) sugar

whipped cream, to serve (optional)

SERVES 8

Gently plunge the fruit in small batches into boiling water for 30 seconds. Remove with a slotted spoon and put in a bowl of iced water. Peel all the fruit except the cherries.

Combine the claret, sherry, sugar and 250 ml (9 fl oz/1 cup) water in a large heavy-based saucepan. Stir over low heat without boiling until the sugar has dissolved. Bring to the boil, reduce the heat and simmer for 5 minutes.

Add the drained fruits to the syrup in small batches and simmer each batch for 5 minutes. Remove with a slotted spoon. Pile the fruit into a bowl. Bring the syrup to the boil, reduce the heat and simmer for a further 5 minutes. Remove from the heat and allow to cool slightly—it should be the consistency of a syrup. Pour over the fruit. Serve with a dollop of freshly whipped cream.

PREPARATION TIME: 40 MINUTES   COOKING TIME: 30 MINUTES

Eastern fruit platter

SANGRIA

1½ tablespoons caster (superfine) sugar
1 tablespoon lemon juice
1 tablespoon orange juice
1 bottle red wine
500 ml (17 fl oz/2 cups) lemonade
(lemon-lime flavoured soda)
2 tablespoons gin
2 tablespoons vodka
1 lemon
1 orange
1 lime
ice cubes, to serve

SERVES 10

Put the caster sugar, lemon juice and orange juice into a large pitcher or bowl and stir until the sugar has dissolved.

Add the red wine, lemonade, gin and vodka. Cut the lemon, orange and lime into halves, remove the seeds and slice all the fruit. Add the slices to the jug and fill with ice. Stir well.

PREPARATION TIME: 10 MINUTES   COOKING TIME: NIL

LEMON AND LIME BARLEY WATER

220 g (7 oz/1 cup) pearl barley
60 ml (2 fl oz/¼ cup) lemon juice
125 ml (4 fl oz/½ cup) lime juice
115 g (4 oz/½ cup) caster (superfine) sugar
ice cubes, to serve
lemon slices, to serve
lime slices, to serve

MAKES ABOUT 1 LITRE (35 FL OZ/4 CUPS)

Boil the barley and 2 litres (70 fl oz/8 cups) water in a large heavy-based saucepan for 30 minutes, or until the liquid has reduced by half. Remove from the heat and strain.

Add the citrus juices and sugar and mix well. Serve chilled with ice, and lemon and lime slices.

PREPARATION TIME: 5 MINUTES +   COOKING TIME: 30 MINUTES

MOROCCAN MINT TEA

1 tablespoon green tea leaves
30 g (1 oz) sugar
1 large handful of spearmint leaves and stalks

SERVES 1

Heat the teapot and add the green tea leaves, sugar and spearmint leaves and stalks. Fill with boiling water and brew for at least 5 minutes. Adjust the sweetness if necessary.

PREPARATION TIME: 5 MINUTES   COOKING TIME: 5 MINUTES

NOTE: In Morocco, this light sweet tea is often served before, and always after every meal, and is prepared at any hour of the day when friends or guests arrive at a Moroccan home. It is sipped in cafés. Traditionally it is served from a silver teapot into ornately painted glasses.

ICED TEA

ice, to serve
125 ml (4 fl oz/½ cup) cold black tea
1 teaspoon sugar
lemon slices, to serve
mint leaves, to serve

SERVES 1

Put ice, cold tea and sugar in a highball glass and stir with a swizzle stick. Garnish with lemon slices and mint leaves.

PREPARATION TIME: 5 MINUTES   COOKING TIME: NIL

NOTE: Iced tea may also be made with cold herbal teas.

Moroccan mint tea

GINGERED WATERMELON JUICE

500 g (1 lb 2 oz) watermelon
2 teaspoons grated fresh ginger
6 ice cubes
wedge of watermelon, to garnish

MAKES 600 ML (21 FL OZ/2$\frac{1}{2}$ CUPS)

Remove the skin and seeds from the watermelon and roughly chop. Put in a blender or food processor with the ginger and process for 2 minutes. Add the ice cubes and process for a further 1 minute, or until the ice is crushed. Serve garnished with a thin wedge of watermelon.

PREPARATION TIME: 5 MINUTES   COOKING TIME: NIL

HOME-MADE LEMONADE

LEMON SYRUP
6 large lemons
6 whole cloves
440 g (15$\frac{1}{2}$ oz/2 cups) sugar

ice cubes, to serve
soda water, to serve
lemon slices, to garnish
mint leaves, to garnish

MAKES ABOUT 1.25 LITRES
(44 FL OZ/5 CUPS)

To make the lemon syrup, slice the lemons and put in a large bowl with the cloves. Cover with 1.25 litres (44 fl oz/5 cups) boiling water. Leave to infuse overnight.

Strain the water into a large saucepan. Discard the lemon slices and cloves. Add the sugar and stir over low heat, without boiling, until dissolved. Bring to the boil and simmer for 10 minutes, or until reduced and slightly syrupy. Allow to cool.

To serve, put ice in a highball glass. Pour over 2 tablespoons lemon syrup and top with soda water. Garnish with lemon slices and mint leaves.

PREPARATION TIME: 10 MINUTES +   COOKING TIME: 15 MINUTES

Gingered watermelon juice

INDEX

INDEX